DEVELOPMENTAL DISABILITIES
OF EARLY CHILDHOOD

DEVELOPMENTAL DISABILITIES OF EARLY CHILDHOOD

Edited by

BARBARA A. FEINGOLD, M.A.

Administrative Director
Little Village School
Merrick, New York

and

CARYL L. BANK, M.S.

Educational Director
Little Village School
Merrick, New York

CHARLES C THOMAS · PUBLISHER
Springfield · Illinois · U.S.A.

Published and Distributed Throughout the World by
CHARLES C THOMAS • PUBLISHER
Bannerstone House
301-327 East Lawrence Avenue, Springfield, Illinois, U.S.A.

© *1978, by* CHARLES C THOMAS • PUBLISHER
ISBN 0-398-03699-3
Library of Congress Catalog Card Number: 77-23035

*With THOMAS BOOKS careful attention is given to all details of
manufacturing and design. It is the Publisher's desire to present
books that are satisfactory as to their physical qualities and artistic
possibilities and appropriate for their particular use. THOMAS
BOOKS will be true to those laws of quality that assure a good
name and good will.*

Printed in the United States of America
N-1

Library of Congress Cataloging in Publication Data

Main entry under title:

Developmental disabilities of early childhood.

    "In April, 1976, the Little Village School for Developmentally Dis-
abled Children and Sagamore Children's Center co-sponsored a professional conference . . . The papers published in this book are based on
proceedings from this conference."
    Includes bibliographies and indexes.
    1. Developmentally disabled children—Congresses.   I. Feingold,
Barbara, A.   II. Bank, Caryl L.   III. Little Village School for
Developmentally Disabled Children.   IV. Sagamore Children's Center.
HV891.D48   362.7'8'3   77-23035

CONTRIBUTORS

CARYL L. BANK, M.S.
Educational Director
Little Village School
Merrick, New York

STELLA CHESS, M.D.
Professor of Child Psychiatry
Director of Child and Adolescent Psychiatry
New York University Medical Center
New York, New York

RALPH COBRINIK, M.D.
Department of Pediatrics
Saint Barnabas Medical Center
Livingston, New Jersey

RICHARD M. COHEN, Ph.D.
Chief Psychologist
Queens Hospital Center
Jamaica, New York

JESSICA G. DAVIS, M.D.
Director of Child Development Center
Chief of Division of Genetics
North Shore University Hospital
Manhasset, New York

BARBARA A. FEINGOLD, M.A.
Administrative Director
Little Village School
Merrick, New York

BRENDA D. GENN, M.S.
Director of Speech Services
Little Village School
Merrick, New York

BRUCE GROSSMAN, Ph.D.
Professor of Early Childhood Education
Hofstra University
Hempstead, New York

MARY HAGAMEN, M.D.
Director of Sagamore Children's Center
Melville, New York

W. D. HITCHINGS, M.D.
The Rappaport Health Research Institute
Quebec, Canada

KENNETH F. KAUFMAN, Ph.D.
Sagamore Children's Center
Melville, New York

PHOEBE LAZARUS, Ed.D.
Supervisor of Special Education
Board of Cooperative Educational Services
Nassau County, New York

ABRAHAM LURIE, Ph.D.
Director of Social Work Services
Long Island Jewish-Hillside Medical Center
New Hyde Park, New York

JOHN M. NEALE, Ph.D.
Department of Psychology
State University of New York at Stony Brook
Stony Brook, New York

CLAIRE SALANT, M.A.
Educational Director
Suffolk Rehabilitation Center
Commack, New York

LEONARD SILVERSTEIN, Ph.D.
United Cerebral Palsy Treatment and
Rehabilitation Center of Nassau County
Roosevelt, New York

SHELDON WEINTRAUB, Ph.D.
Department of Psychology
State University of New York at Stony Brook
Stony Brook, New York

BARBARA C. WILSON, Ph.D.
Neuropsychology Section
Department of Psychology
North Shore University Hospital
Manhasset, New York
The Department of Neurology
Cornell University Medical Center
New York, New York

JAMES J. WILSON, Ph.D.
Department of Psychology
Queens College
City University of New York
New York, New York
Preschool Development Program
North Shore University Hospital
Manhasset, New York

PREFACE

In April, 1976, the Little Village School for Developmentally Disabled Children and Sagamore Children's Center cosponsored a professional conference, "Developmental Disabilities of Early Childhood." A unique blending of many disciplines was achieved. The papers published in this book are based on proceedings from this conference. The editors would like to take this opportunity to thank all the participating authors for their outstanding contributions.

It is hoped that the knowledge and research presented in this book will serve to further the needs of the developmentally disabled child and his family.

CARYL BANK
BARBARA FEINGOLD

INTRODUCTION

EARLY INTERVENTION
IN DEVELOPMENTAL DISABILITIES:

A Job For Everyone

MARY HAGAMEN, M.D.

*It was six men of Indostan to learning much in-
    clined
Who went to see the elephant (although all of them
    were blind)
That each by observation might satisfy his mind.*

JOHN GODFREY SAXE   1818-1887

THOUGH fifty years is scarcely an eyeblink in the recorded history of the world, during this time the medical community
has gained a greater majority of the present knowledge of the
pathology that affects man.

The field of medicine has moved from looking only at disease
to looking at health and what measures are necessary for its pre-
servation. Of necessity, this calls attention to groups of apparently normal people who, from their constitutional and social history,
are about to develop a particular ailment. The medical field
abounds with screening programs focused on persons who are
high risk. Populations that are high risk for hypertension, dia-
betes, lung cancer, and coronary artery disease, etc. have been
delineated. Such programs are aimed at finding an illness in its
asymptomatic prodromal stages, so that intervention can begin
before there is any debility. Another important function of
screening programs is helping people understand the factors, components of their life-style and environment, that tend to exacer-

bate any heredity predisposition to a disease in themselves.

Today, educational programs help the layman realize the role of heredity and its interaction with environmental factors, such as diet, smoking, and drinking. These are bonafide components of public health programs.

Certainly, the seeds of the hereditary-environmental philosophy seem to fall on the most fertile of soils in the field of obstetrics and pediatrics, where, theoretically, there is the longest period of time with the most strategically placed fulcrum to utilize the energies of the medical profession in preventing disease and disabilities. Although dramatic battles have already been won on this frontier through our understanding and intervention in such conditions as Rh incompatibility and phenylketonuria, much pioneer work remains to be done. Perhaps the most enigmatic among the problems of children are those classified as *developmental disabilities*. These problems lie in the territory where professional responsibility overlaps with that of the disciplines such as education, law, social services, and the clergy. Very often preventive measures suggested through advances in medical technology are incompatible with social and religious values. Bioethics has become an important topic of discussion among all those interested in promoting the "good life" and the "pursuit of happiness."

Because of the overlapping of professional responsibility among the various disciplines that deal with children, there is an enormous potential for confusion that can be likened to the blind man who so diligently studied the elephant.

If we are to apply all that we know about the prevention of developmental disabilities, whether it is in the primary, secondary, or tertiary level of preventive care, it is necessary first to coordinate the knowledge and services of those specialists and subspecialists within the medical profession: general practitioners, geneticists, obstetricians, neonatalogists, pediatricians, and child psychiatrists.

There is a need for interdisciplinary understanding within the limited fields of psychology and education. Interchanges must work between behavioralists and analysts. Teachers at a level of kindergarten through college must understand both their own role in educating the average youngster and the variety and forms of special education.

Some of the fiercest prejudices exist at an interdisciplinary level in all fields. Psychology, education, and medicine each have denominations within their ranks. If we are to do well with the developmentally disabled, we must create programs of enlightenment geared to illuminating facts, not fads, as well as the opportunities for dialogues between all those interested. If this can be accomplished, many prejudices will be reduced, if not erased. Social services to children and families need to be free of the cumbersome bureaucratic entanglements that discourage many marginally needy people from the services for which they are eligible.

Perhaps most important, there needs to be a cross–fertilization between the traditional human services fields (health, education, and welfare) and the legal profession. No one disagrees that the rights of children in the United States are a basic heritage deserving of protection, but something has gone wrong when the rights of the child are pitted against the rights of the parents in litigation. Lawyers eager to defend a valid philosophy sometimes intensify the complex problems they have set out to ameliorate.

On the other hand, service-oriented professionals working with another set of facts are apt to develop a religiosity that rigidly resists compromise. Well-meaning parents can be caught in the middle with the poor understanding of their child, rights, and responsibilities.

If the battle against developmental disabilities is to progress, it will be necessary to overcome intra– and interdisciplinary differences in the creation of a master plan that provides for dialogue at every step of the way — a dialogue that diffuses information to such a degree that it, in essence, acts to remove the blindfolds on the wise men who are so carefully examining the elephant of developmental disabilities. For on this frontier, there is a job for everyone — doctor, lawyer, teacher, social worker, scientist, student, child-care worker, and, most of all, the informed consumer — the parent.

Human development, as defined by Meier,[4] refers to "a change in a person's function or capacity in any one or combination of four interacting domains; physical, emotional, social and intellectual." Development is distinguished from growth. *Growth* relates primarily to change in size or quantity, whereas *development* relates more to change in function or quality.

The human baby is dependent upon a variety of factors to support optimum development. There must be:

1. A normal genetic endowment
2. An insult-free, ten-month intrauterine life
3. A nontraumatic birth
4. A consistent, loving, stimulating environment safe from infections and accidents

With these attributes, a child can usually be assured of life without a developmental disability.

However, despite the rapid increase in technology and man's control of nature in the twentieth century, it is increasingly difficult to assure every baby born the attributes for normal development.

As a result of technology, the lives of more babies who have had insults to their nervous system, *in utero* or at birth, have been saved. However, children who in earlier times would have died in infancy because of anatomic or physiologic deficits are being given a good chance for a normal life expectancy through the advent of surgical and biochemical intervention. Yet, we are increasingly less able than preceding generations to assure babies of a living, stimulating, and safe environment maintained by an intact marriage and supported by an extended family. Thus, in the last quarter of the twentieth century, there seem to be increasing numbers of children with developmental disabilities of both a major and minor nature. The major disabilities are usually associated with moderate and severe mental retardation, while the minor disabilities affecting far greater numbers of children are reflected as mild retardation and learning disabilities.

Another way of looking at developmental disabilities is by analyzing their roots of origin; that is whether the handicap is *intraindividual,* resulting from a constitutional deficit within the individual, or whether the handicap is the result of an *experiential* deficit having its origin in the environment.

Examples of intraindividual problems are demonstrated by children who —

1. Have a genetic deficit, i.e. Down's syndrome, PKU, etc.
2. Traumatic uterine sojourn, i.e. babies born to mothers who have had rubella in early pregnancy or
3. Have been premature, traumatized at birth, or suffered infections or accidents early in life

The developmental disabilities *individual* in origin, are those secondary to the experiences that the child had in the critical pre-school years. A multitude of investigators[1,3,5] have shown that over two-thirds of "slow learners" and "school failures" are retarded on the basis of experiential deprivation frequently associated with the "culture of poverty." Although such children are physically intact, they have a developmental deficit that is as real and disabling a problem as any of the more grossly identified disabilities. Because of the much larger number of such individuals, their handicap has a more profound and devastating effect on our social system. Although the causes that are clearly intra– and extraindividual in their roots of origin can be isolated, what is happening in the individual child is more difficult to define. The past decades of observation have shown that the child reacts on his environment to a greater degree than formerly was believed possible. Under closer scrutiny, some conditions that were frequently blamed on parent behaviors have turned out to be only reactions to the primary problem in the child. The prime example of this finding is the condition known as *autism.* By the same token, some children who have been subject to severe deprivation of a devastating degree seem to have come through such experiences only to excell among their peers. Developmental disabilities in children represent a complex of actions and reactions both intra– and extraindividual in origin.

Today, it is only the more severe conditions related to cerebral palsy and retardation that are thought of under the designation of developmental disabilities. However, as we begin to organize a system for identifying children who have mild to moderate disabilities of mixed intra– and extraindividual origin, the numbers of children eligible for developmental disability resources may increase up to tenfold and will present an interdisciplinary challenge.

Because of the massive social implications of increasing numbers of experientially handicapped individuals, President Lyndon B. Johnson's administration initiated Project Head Start as a major part of the war on poverty in the mid-1960s. This heroic nationwide effort to overcome the results of early cultural deprivation on educational development of children in the poverty cycle was too large and uneven in the quality of implementation to be properly evaluated. It was not as effective as many had hoped, but it was a critical milestone in calling the attention of all persons interested in children to the potential value of early childhood programs.

In the field of education, investigators had been looking long and hard at what determinants of development in a child's life could be manipulated to overcome the developmental disabilities that were extraindividual in origin.[6]

At the same time, leaders in the field of education for the handicapped had been working to discover how they could create an environment for the child with a handicap of intraindividual origin that would minimize his deficits.

One of the lessons evident from Project Head Start was the need for intervention to begin before the preschool period in order to be maximally effective. The United States government followed this lead with the initiation of the Parent and Child Development Centers, aimed at helping parents understand and participate in the enrichment program for their children. The vital role of parents was recognized initially through programs designed to provide early intervention for children disabled by extraindividual cause. However, application of the principle of parent involvement plays an even greater role in the lives of children who have a developmental disability of intraindividual origin.

Although the seed of the parent-professional partnership was born in the field of early childhood education, it was rapidly disseminated to those interested in education of the handicapped. For some readers, there may seem to be nothing new in this concept. For years, there has been a kind of parent-professional partnership between teachers and parents as evidenced by the Parent-Teacher Association (PTA) chartered more than half a century earlier. However, this began when the child was five or six years old and was often more a social liaison than a working relationship in which parents participated in teaching. In more recent years, parents have often been sharply discouraged from becoming involved in the teaching of reading and other educational skills to their offspring.

As results are compiled from programs in which the goal is to increasingly involve parents in verbal interaction with their children, it is becoming evident that early intervention in developmental disabilities of an extraindividual type can best be done in a home, with a mother who has a close relationship with some type of parent support center administered by professionals. In the same vein, investigators, such as Weikert Fraiberg have shown that to minimize the intraindividual developmental disability, it is necessary to provide a program in which the mother or another member of the child's family is taught to understand and participate in a home-based, infant-stimulation program.

Intervention involves developing a system that will provide the mother with emotional support, as well as guidance in how to play and talk with her baby. If a newborn baby is known to be in a high-risk category, or if there is a known birth defect, it is ideal to enroll the child and mother at once in an infant-intervention project. Although such programs are now few and far between, they are increasing in number across the country and within the next decade should be as available as were kindergartens thirty years ago. Because of the low incidence of birth defects, it will always be hard to provide direct service to parents of handicapped children in sparsely populated areas. However, the increasing electronic technology may help resolve some of the isolation of these families.

It has been shown that a system of services that can provide the mother and father with information and understanding of their child's condition, as well as emotional support necessary to help them work through the feelings about their child, is essential in early intervention. It is also important that the parent be trained by those experienced in the specific care of the infant with a developmental disability. In order to accomplish this training, physicians have turned to teachers and psychologists to forge the link necessary for early intervention and a parent-professional partnership. Effective programs usually encompass a psychologist, nurse, and teacher who work to educate, train, and support parents in providing the care and stimulation necessary in early intervention.

When intervention is done, it has been shown that the child with extraindividual handicaps develops in a way comparable to his middle-class peers, and furthermore, contrasts the gains made by Head Start children. These gains are retained when mothers are provided with understanding, attention, and support in a program that encompasses videophone and training by T.V. cassettes. This program enables parents to learn to enjoy and to interact with their babies. With children whose handicap is of intraindividual origin there are also gains, not the least of which is the satisfaction of the parents in knowing that they are participating and contributing useful information to their youngster's treatment plans. As often happens, programs that involve parents in the home are the most effective. From a monetary standpoint, they are the most efficient, having a cost effectiveness far superior to intervention programs that depend on bringing the child out of the home and into a child-care center.

Summary

Early intervention in developmental disabilities is dependent upon the origination of a master plan that provides for a co-ordinated effort by a wide variety of professionals, in combination with consumers, to work together to assure that every baby born has the opportunity to develop to the full level of his or her potential.

Cooperation at both intra– and interdisciplinary levels is essential if all the information presently available in early intervention programs is to be utilized.

No program can be successful without the involvement of the parent or those who are the child's primary caretaker (s) . In contrast to earlier programs of parent involvement where parents were seen to be counseled, the new intervention programs seek to have the parents as active partners to the professional in implementing an organized plan that assures the optimum development of their child.

REFERENCES

1. Bloom, B.S.: *Stability and Change in Human Characteristics.* New York, Wiley, 1964.
2. Hunt, J.McV.: *Intelligence and Experience.* New York, Ronald, 1961.
3. Masland, R.L., Saranson, S.B., and Gladwin, T.: *Mental Subnormality.* New York, Basic, 1958.
4. Meier, J.H.: Cognitive development: Mental retardation. In Johnston, R. and Magrab, P. (Eds.): *Developmental Disorders: Assessment, Treatment, Education.* Baltimore, Univ Park, 1976.
5. Riessman, F.: *The Culturally Deprived Child.* New York, Har-Row, 1962.
6. White, B.L.: An experimental approach to the effects of experience on early human behavior. In Hill, J.P. (Ed.): *Minnesota Symposia on Child Psychology.* Minneapolis, U of Minn Pr, 1967.

CONTENTS

DEVELOPMENTAL DISABILITIES
OF EARLY CHILDHOOD

CHAPTER 1.

AN INTRODUCTION TO DEVELOPMENTAL DISABILITIES

STELLA CHESS, M.D.

A GENERAL term such as *developmental disabilities* can be very useful or can be used in a virtually meaningless way. In its meaningful version, it is a beginning statement that can provide the starting point for careful analysis and lead to proper decisions. These decisions range as far apart as periodic assessment only to a multifaceted program of sequential stimulation over a long period of time. In its least productive use, *developmental disabilities* has been used as an umbrella term, which obfuscates the actual problems of the child, squeezes him into a program ill-suited to his developmental needs, and temporarily — very temporarily — nurtures the illusion that a child with a serious limitation will, in the end, be capable of functioning within ordinary circumstances and able to withstand ordinary interpersonal demands and stresses.

The most important colleagues of the professionals involved in identifying the deviant child's specific difficulties are the parents. Whatever immediate reactions they may have had to the first suspicion that their child was not developing normally and no matter what defensive patterns they may have employed to cope with their feelings, guilt, denial, blame, or anger, etc., parents try to mobilize their energies to cooperate with a meaningful search into the causes and nature of the problem. If treated like intelligent individuals, whose expert knowledge of the minute details of their child's functioning in different situations is the basic material for mapping out the child's developmental deviances, they will be expert coworkers. They have the basic information that permits assessment of an upward rate of movement in separate developmental areas, as well as recognition of the youngster's strengths and abilities. Most parents, once over the fear that the investigation is simply for the purpose of labeling and, hence, excluding their child from existing facilities, can become coeducators who can reinforce at home those patterns being introduced in special programs during the formal educative portion of the child's day.

As a summary, what must be ascertained in such an evaluation is reviewed. The basic distinction is that between temporary delay, as opposed to more permanent defect. The proposal to evaluate all preschoolers for developmental status, while introduced with positive intent, has its worrisome side. There are many variations in rates of development which, in the very early years, are not easy to identify clearly as such. Without longitudinal study, these may, in the earliest appearance, be indistinguishable from more serious and permanent defects. Early identification of temporary developmental delay, if incorrectly labelled as a defect, may result in excluding such a child from the normative educational track, and because of under– or inappropriate stimulation, may in fact lead to a self-fulfilling prophesy. It becomes necessary, therefore, to check such a child at regular periodic intervals, during which it becomes possible to note whether the area of delay is showing acceleration of development, is remaining as far behind proportionately as when first observed, or is becoming even more deviant.

WHAT TO OBSERVE

While children, even in early infancy, have a wide repertoire of competencies, for the sake of useful focus, these can be placed in several major categories: motor, visual, affective, linguistic, and social-adaptive. If descriptive data on each of these are noted down, both as they occur in formal examination and as they are observed during ordinary daily activity, it becomes possible to check these over time in several ways. First, is the behavior that occurs in each area, age-appropriate or ahead of the age or behind? Or is it deviant in a manner that is not age-specific but rather would be abnormal at any age? Even though such questions may not be able to be answered through a single recording of functioning at a given evaluation, a careful, written description permits comparison at a later evaluation, when it may be more possible to see if and in what direction significant change is occurring.

While the intellectual level of the child will make a crucial difference in his/her ability to make use of a planned program, it cannot be observed directly but will be able to be estimated in terms of the total adaptive picture, as well as through formal testing, where this is suited to the youngster's sensory and motor capabilities.

Normative milestones exist in each of these areas. However, under certain circumstances, such milestones may be misleading. Direct effects of disabilities are well recognized. It is generally realized, for example, that a significant degree of hearing loss would interfere with linguistic development, even though the child were intellectually normal and had adequate motor control of the muscles of the larynx, lips, cheeks, and tongue. However, cross-over effects of disabilities must also be accounted for, if the significance of some delays are to be comprehended. Blind children will be delayed in their early acquisition of motor skills and will sit, stand, and walk at later age than seeing children. The visualization of the world around them, the interesting objects held out, the desired persons reaching out their arms — all act as stimuli to children to lift up the head for better visualization, to sit, to reach, or to crawl in order to be near the beckoning person, place, or thing. A visually defective child who shows a delay in motor skills does not necessarily have an organismic problem in the motor area. Similarly, deaf children cannot interact fully with the speaking and hearing people around them. Consequently, they will be retarded in adaptive skills. They cannot argue, push limits, or ask questions. In short, they cannot have the usual learning experiences through which the finer points of adaptation are mastered, unless those about them are skilled in manual language, thus tapping intact visual competence for communication. As a further example of cross-over effect, the youngster with significant motor impairment may be behind in speech despite having no hearing difficulty, since other children and adults tend to avoid interactions when their usual modes of interplay are barred. This will be especially true if the child's own speech is hard to comprehend. In thalidomide children, there is the problem of limb absence or deformity making interactive play most difficult; caretakers often thus limit their time with the child to that required by basic nurturing necessities. Failing to hear much speech, such children are deprived of equal opportunity to learn speaking patterns and skills.

Such cross-over factors, if not borne in mind, may lead to an incorrect interpretation of correctly perceived facts. With an unusual cause for experiential deprivation, *inability* may be assumed to be *disability*. The program devised for such a child may be insufficient and incorrect for his/her capacities for development.

To summarize, developmental evaluation involves the following steps: (1) Describe what the child is doing in the major developmental areas. (2) Monitor every three to six months with descriptions that provide comparability. (3) Flesh out the formal examination by recording functioning within the naturalistic environment. (4) Develop a longitudinal picture of the patterns of competence in the major areas.

The outcome of evaluation may be the definition of ways in which the child's environment must be altered. In addition to inclusion in a special program, such changes may also involve basic changes in home management and stimulation. To criticize parental handling in this way is distinctly not equivalent to passing a negative judgment on them. Without a constructive critique of the daily demands and stimuli that parents were including in their handling of the child that had been previously offered, one can hardly expect them to determine that which the experts are finding difficult to define.

The first step after having decided what must be done for the child, or even what must be tried out as a therapeutic experiment, is to lay out a careful plan to be monitored, reassessed, and redecided periodically between professionals and parents. If changed handling is suggested for reasons which can be explained, and parental reportage is scheduled as part of a regular evaluatory mechanism, then parents will not feel scolded or blamed. Then, cooperative interplay between family and professionals for the benefit of the child will be enhanced.

Of the various defects that occur, affective lack on the part of the child is perhaps the most difficult for parents to deal with. Parent-infant interaction is enormously dependent on mutual feedback. To expect mothers and fathers to supply warmth and stimuli of all kinds to an apparently unresponsive and disinterested child is to demand something that professionals would find enormously taxing. It may be a good rule for professionals to picture for themselves how they would go about carrying out a recommendation before making it to parents.

CHAPTER 2.

A MODEL ECLECTIC PROGRAM FOR THE EDUCATION OF YOUNG DEVELOPMENTALLY DISABLED CHILDREN

CARYL L. BANK, M.S.
BARBARA A. FEINGOLD, M.A.
BRENDA D. GENN, M.S.

L ITTLE Village School is a structured therapeutic day school for children aged two and one-half to ten, who have been diagnosed as mentally retarded, emotionally disturbed, neurologically impaired, minimally brain damaged, or multiply handicapped. It is a nonprofit, nondiscriminatory school chartered by the Board of Regents of the State of New York. The children who attend Little Village School represent all socioeconomic levels and reside within the geographic confines of Nassau County. They come from varied religious, racial, and ethnic backgrounds. The school was founded in 1969, at which time there were limited facilities in Nassau County, New York, for the education of developmentally disabled preschoolers.

Little Village School is a unique educational facility. It was the first school in Nassau County to deliberately group and educate children according to their developmental levels, rather than diagnostic categories. This innovative approach to grouping deemphasized the labeling of children and focused upon their functioning. A vital aspect of the Little Village philosophy is parent education and involvement. The communication between home and school is accomplished through the provision of ongoing workshops, group meetings, counseling, and a general open-door policy. Little Village advocates total committment toward the child and his family.

The primary sources of referral to Little Village are clinics, hospitals, private practitioners, and mental health agencies. After a referral has been made, the family then files an application with the school. The child's medical and psychological records are forwarded, and an interview is arranged for the child and his parents. At this interview, the philosophy of the school is explained to the parents, and they are taken on a tour of the facilities. While the social worker is conferring with the parents, the child is being evaluated and assessed by the staff psychologist. Upon completion of this intake procedure, the staff then confers as to the availability of appropriate placement for the child, and a decision is made accordingly.

Little Village School is in session five days a week on a year-round basis. Children up through the age of five years attend classes three hours a day; older children attend five hours. Students who remain in school at noon enjoy a cold lunch program. Door-to-door transportation is provided for each child through arrangements made by their home school district. Once a child has been accepted to Little Village, he is placed in a class that will best meet his individual needs. The etiology of his problem is considered secondarily to the educational and therapeutic remediation of his symptoms. Classes are comprised of seven children, a certified special education teacher, and an assistant teacher.

Little Village School uses a special curriculum specifically designed to meet the needs of developmentally disabled youngsters. This curriculum provides for a sequential order of developmental skills encompassing the following areas: gross motor, fine motor, social, self-help, cognitive, and language skills.

In the area of gross motor skills, specific experiences are provided for the development, awareness, and control of body parts, spatial relations, movement, balance, and coordination. Fine motor skills include activities such as grasping, tracking, manipulation of textures and materials, and hand-eye coordination activities. These psycho– and perceptual-motor techniques are an integral part of each child's daily routine. A consultant physical therapist assists in coordinating these programs.

The areas of social and self-help skills provide for adequate functioning in daily life experiences. Activities include: an awareness of self, relating to others, sharing, listening, task completion, behavioral control, and awareness of common dangers. Also included are toileting, feeding, eating, drinking, personal care, and dressing. The above skills are an integral part of the curriculum, because they are necessary prerequisites for independence, even within a custodial situation.

Cognition training is an aspect of the curriculum where boundaries fall within all other areas. Cognitive skills are the higher processes of learning in which each child proceeds at his or her own rate. Various activities that encourage the acquisition of these skills include following directions, recognition and naming of objects, matching, categorizing, discriminating, auditory training, and conceptual understanding. Individual goals are planned in sequential gradations that strengthen receptive abilities and continue on to encourage the higher thought processes.

Language skills are inherent in all areas of the curriculum. The speech and language services afforded the children at Little Village School are enumerated in a later section of this chapter.

All sensory modalities are stimulated and developed throughout all learning areas. All learning areas are synthesized into an ongoing experience, specific to each child's needs. The curriculum as described above was created so that each child may achieve his maximum potential in all areas of development within his total environment (Fig. 2-1).

CURRICULUM IMPLEMENTATION

The first few weeks of the school year are spent assessing and evaluating each child's developmental levels. A profile is made of each child's specific abilities in all curriculum areas. The teachers use these composites as a basis for planning individual and group goals. The children's achievements are carefully monitored through a system of daily charting. The classroom teacher and assistant teacher confer with the educational director every two weeks. At these meetings, each child's progress is individually reviewed. A determination is then made regarding the goals and activities appropriate for the next two weeks. The

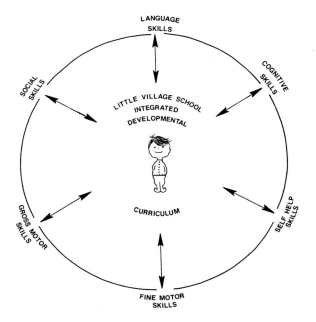

Figure 2-1.

curriculum is implemented by each classroom teacher through a highly structured program (Table 2-I) .

It is believed that children who exhibit developmental delays especially require firm boundaries and carefully defined limits, in order to function to their optimum potential. The atmosphere in the classroom is one of acceptance and warmth. Positive reinforcement is utilized to encourage desirable behavior. This consists of edible and social rewards being given to promote stimulus-response efficacy. This behaviorally oriented psychoeducational treatment facilitates learning in a supportive environment.

Speech and language services are an essential aspect of the total prescriptive program at the Little Village School. Language stimulation and training programs are prepared for each child, both on an individual and group basis. The principle component of oral communication, the development of a verbal code for

TABLE 2-I

SAMPLE DAILY TIME SCHEDULE FOR LITTLE VILLAGE SCHOOL

8:30-9:00	Teachers and assistant teachers prepare for day's activities
9:00-9:15	Children enter school (nondirected play until all children arrive)
9:15-9:45	Group morning activities (socialization, self-help skills, body awareness) Activities: attendance taking, songs, rhythm band, mirror work
9:45-10:15	Bathroom (group): toileting, grooming, bathroom safety
10:15-10:45	Individualized prescriptive activities (fine motor) Activities: peg board, stringing beads, building cubes, cutting
10:45-11:15	Gross motor skills (group): physical education program
11:15-11:45	Individualized prescriptive activities (cognitive) Activities: auditory training, following simple directions
11:45-12:15	Lunch (group) Activities: cooling, self-help skills, socialization
12:15-12:30	Rest time
12:30-1:00	Individualized prescriptive activities (cognitive) Activity: visual perception, tracking integration of audiovisual materials
1:00-1:30	Group language lesson (language development) conducted by speech therapist
1:30-1:45	Bathroom (group): toileting, grooming
1:45-2:00	Preparation for going home Activity: self-help skills, dressing
2:00-2:30	Teachers and assistant teachers' review and record the day's progress

receptive and expressive language, is applied. Each child is guided through a language development program specific to his individual needs. This program is implemented by two full-time certified speech therapists, who assess cognitive, prelinguistic, and linguistic abilities of the children and set specific goals for language skills. The program begins with preverbal training when necessary, and includes a multisensory approach encompassing all areas of expressive and receptive language training.

Each child receives individual language therapy twice a week and is involved in a weekly group, language- stimulation setting within his classroom. The children, through working in a group, learn to acquire, sort, integrate, and use verbal information. A speech therapist conducts the group lessons, and the classroom teachers are active participants. This group language lesson stimulates and strengthens expressive language, while developing the realization of the need for language skills in communication. This also reinforces the strengths achieved in individual therapy. Consultation between the speech clinicians and the classroom teacher are held monthly to discuss each child's progress in the area of language and to suggest situations in the classroom in which practice can reinforce language skills.

Parent education and involvement is a vital part of the speech and language program at Little Village. Parents are involved in weekly meeting workshops whereby therapeutic techniques of language stimulation and training for home carryover are taught and discussed. There is ongoing communication and close involvement in the child's speech program. These programs facilitate the transfer of the child's language development from school to his total environment.

The Little Village staff includes a full-time school psychologist and two consulting clinical psychologists. These professionals work directly with other staff members and families. The children are individually assessed to ascertain their cognitive and affective functioning. They are also observed in the classroom. Recommendations for treatment and remediation are discussed at staff conferences. Parents are seen individually to provide understanding of their child's problems and to be made cognizant of the psychoeducational techniques employed by the school. One member of the psychological staff is always available, including after-school hours, in the event of a crisis situation.

The psychological staff offers various types of parent education workshops. This is in consideration of the fact that some parents prefer large-group meetings whereas others are more comfortable in a small-group setting. Little Village School offers to all families several short-term workshops that are specific in nature: These deal with such topics as toilet training and feeding. Other workshops led by a clinical psychologist meet regularly for an extended period of time. Here, a small group of parents are brought together for an indepth group counseling experience. Everyone is afforded the opportunity to participate in a workshop series of this type. There are parent meetings held monthly during school hours, to which all are welcome. These meetings are less formal and provide the opportunity for parents to get acquainted with each other and to benefit from and exchange ideas and experiences. It has been found that the availability of a wide range of psychological services enable parents to gain insight and support in living with their developmentally disabled child.

Communication between the school and home is enhanced in many ways. Little Village School has an open-door policy whereby parents are welcome to visit the school and see the program in progress. Grandparents and siblings are specifically invited to share special days at the school. Individual parent-teacher conferences and parent-director conferences are held periodically throughout the year. Daily communication with parents is achieved as the youngsters bring home notes from school explaining a highlight of their day. Parents are then asked to reciprocate by sending notes to school concerning their child's after-school experiences.

It is important that the public is educated to the needs of the developmentally disabled child. Little Village School serves as a demonstration center and training facility for student teachers in special education. The school is affiliated with Hofstra and Adelphi Universities, C. W. Post College, and State University of New York at Farmingdale. High school students from neighboring communities participate in a cooperative work-study program at Little Village. The Little Village School staff are available to address interested community groups. Conferences such as the one this book is based upon exemplify community outreach. It is only through education and knowledge of the needs of these children that the community-at-large will respond with its full support of programs.

Little Village School is a special place for a special child. It is the beginning of an educational journey: Most children who leave Little Village go onto special education classes in the various public school programs of Nassau County. This represents a major achievement for these youngsters, whose initial prognosis was unfavorable. It has been successfully demonstrated at Little Village School that early intervention can have a dramatic effect upon the lives of developmentally disabled children.

CHAPTER 3.

LEARNING DISABILITIES: THE ROLE OF THE PEDIATRICIAN; EVALUATIONS OF PATIENTS AND FAMILIES

RALPH COBRINIK, M.D.

THE CONCEPT of *learning disability* holds varying connotations for different disciplines and even for workers within the same discipline. Furthermore, there is a wide range of opinion, both intra– and extramurally, as to what role the pediatric community should play in diagnosis and treatment of this disorder. This chapter attempts to review the literature and draw conclusions that, hopefully, will serve to clarify some of these issues.

Learning disability is one of those many vague, jargon-like terms that has evolved during the past three decades. It is the *unexpected* failure of a child to attain academic success in spite of a lack of any obvious reason. Kinsbourne[1] stressed the word *unexpected*. Mental retardation, gross neurological impairment, psychotic disorders, severe visual and auditory deficits, and the effects of a malignant environmental or educational experience should not be included. These factors are expected to prevent learning and, indeed, do. This article addresses itself to the child who enters school with the expectation that she will succeed, yet does not: She *underachieves*. His/her problems are subtle and require evaluation and appropriate treatment.

PEDIATRIC ROLE

What is the role of the medical profession, and particularly, the pediatrician, in the evaluation and treatment of learning disabilities? No other group of physicians has been more active and introspective than pediatricians in coming to grips with their future role. McQueen[2] emphasized this point at the American Academy of Pediatrics Annual Meeting in 1975. This is particularly true when dealing in an area that is already established domain of other disciplines, such as in learning disabilities. Many pediatricians become self-conscious, even defensive, when confronted by educators and psychologists, etc. But, indeed, it is the right and duty of pediatricians to involve themselves in learning disabilities. When one considers the scope and frequency of learning problems in their patients, perhaps in 10 percent, can pediatricians afford *not* to get involved? With planned limitation of family size, parents now, more than ever, are concerned with the quality of the product in which they are investing so much of themselves.

In the past four years, there has been a barrage of articles and letters of rebuttal in the pediatric literature that attempts to define and modify the pediatric role in learning disabilities. The wide range of opinions emphasizes the controversy that exists. Garrard[3] seems to be saying that pediatricians had better abrogate their classical role of total comprehensive child care when it comes to learning disabilities. They should be involved exclusively in the biomedical aspects of prevention, recognition of sensory deficits, and identification of pertinent historical, genetic, neurological, and syndromic factors. He feels other aspects of the child's educational problems are more germane to other disciplines and do not really involve the pediatrician.

Studies reported by Kenny and Clemmens[4,5] indicate that the medical, electroencephalographic, and neurological aspects of the evaluation of children with learning disabilities contribute little to the understanding of their learning problems, because of the negative findings usually obtained. However, the authors' lack of appreciation of the significance of "negative findings"; the design of their studies, which include multiple developmental problems and a preponderance of mental retardation; and their failure to appreciate the pediatrician's role as the child's and family's "advocate", particularly when dealing with school authorities, brought on justly deserved criticisms in letters to the editor.[6-8]

More recently, Schour and Clemmens[9] questioned whether,

even if the medical clinic workup is multidisciplined, the school would follow the recommendations. Their study shows that recommendations were implemented in 85 percent of the cases if school personnel participated in the evaluation conference, but only in 57 percent of the cases if the information was transmitted by letter alone.

In 1971, The American Academy of Pediatrics Committee on Children with Handicaps[10] assumed that the pediatrician is the logical professional responsible for the learning disabled child. McQueen[2] sees this as one of pediatric's major roles of the future. However, Menkes[11] indicates that pediatricians, as well as child neurologists and psychiatrists, may not be adequately prepared for this role and have often, therefore, abrogated it to others in the school system. His suggested solution was to have a school-based physician trained in child developmental and educational problems, a subspecialty of educational pediatrics. This view was endorsed by Asbed, Fox, and Wender.[12]

Needless to say, the school-based physician proposal also produced controversy in the pediatric community, which questioned where a school physician's primary loyalties would reside, what relations he would have with the child's physician,[12,13] and whether this would lead to too-early overdiagnosis and overtreatment.[14]

Another response[15] to Menkes indicated that, in view of its prevalence and importance, every pediatrician must be adequately trained in this area. Furthermore, it was asked whether subspecialization and its almost certain subsequent drive for certification would limit the role of the general pediatrician, who may already have a special interest and talent in this area.

Perhaps the most significant indication of an awakening of consciousness in the medical community is demonstrated by the change in attitude of the pediatric neurologists. For a long time, many of them shied away from "learning disabilities."[11] However, at The Second Annual Meeting of the Child Neurology Society in Nashville in 1973, its president[16] and some of its most distinguished founders stressed the importance of members' involvement in developmental problems.

It would seem that these divergent views could be unified by an eclectic approach. First, there is a definite need for a close primary doctor-patient relationship. This should and does not have to be abandoned because other professionals, such as the developmental neurologist, psychologist, and educator, etc., become involved. It is no different than sharing responsibility with a dermatologist or surgeon. However, general pediatric training programs must begin to stress developmental neurology in their curricula. Pediatricians must then be prepared to spend the time and energy in applying this new-found knowledge.

Second, there is also a real need for a physician who specializes in developmental problems, particularly for more difficult diagnostic and therapeutic cases. He should serve as a consultant to and, indeed, a leader of school and agency child-study teams in order to serve the individual child, as well as to develop appropriate programs for the learning disabled and other handicapped children. It is probably wiser if his function is independent of the school system, so that his primary advocacy remains child-oriented. Chamberlin[17] went a step further. He sees this special pediatrician specifically trained and involved primarily in the area of basic child development. Part of this function would be to train general pediatricians and medical students in all aspects of child development and its aberrations.

Past experience has taught that the medical profession must never again abrogate its responsibility. Although physicians recognize and appreciate the enormous contributions of the social, behavioral, and educational sciences while "resting on the sidelines," one wonders if some of the "voodoo" in terminology, diagnosis, and treatment that has become entrenched in some of these disciplines, and others, could have been avoided if pediatrics had been more vigilant.

The medical profession is by no means free of guilt. One need not go further than a local T.V. channel, magazine, or copy of the *New York Times*[18] to see physicians report and support poorly documented statements. Frank and Levinson[19] developed multiple hypotheses concerning the relationship of dyslexia to cerebellar-vestibular dysfunction and reported the value of their machine in diagnosing preschool dyslexia. Conclusions are reached with little reported evidence or documentation.

"Patterning" to develop "neurological organization" in children with various neurological and learning problems has been practiced for almost two decades on possibly thousands of children.[20,21] However, documented studies to indicate any efficacy are still lacking.[22-26]

Optometric eye exercises enjoy a wide popularity.[27,28] Yet, the joint organizational statement of The American Academy of Pediatrics, The American Academy of Ophthalmology and Otolaryngology, and The American Association of Ophthalmology,[29] as well as The International Ophthalmological Seminar,[30] indicate the lack of validity in such "therapy." Volumes by Kephart[31] and Barsch[32] devoted to motor exercises as a means of ameliorating learning disabilities are still to be put into perspective and adequately evaluated for validity. When visual-perception training programs like the Frostig[33] program were put to the test by Church,[34] Bishop,[35] and Pitcher-Baker,[36] their validity was found wanting. Then there are diets,[37,38] multivitamins,[38] caffeine,[39] and trace metals,[40] all vying for recognition. Grossman,[41] among others, finds insufficient evidence to support any of these "therapeutic" regimes.

Learning disabled children must get back to the business of schools: "the three Rs." That is where amelioration must be obtained. It is the pediatric community's responsibility to see that standard pedagogy is replaced only by systems that show documented merit, rather than by whims.

THE EVALUATION

Inherent in *evaluation* is its implication for treatment. Garrard[3] put it succinctly when he stated, "Recognize that the purposes of evaluation are inseparable from the objectives of intervention."

A full circle has been drawn: What started out years ago as an amorphous, nebulous concept of learning problems subsequently developed into "labelmanship" with a vengence. The more sophisticated the professional discipline or the state special education code,[42] the more lengthy and obscure are the diagnostic classifications. Presently, however, Bateman[43] and others reject the idea that a "diagnostic label" is necessary or even desirable in educational handicaps. Behavioral therapy for functional deficits, they claim, regardless of origin, is all that is necessary. Labels do have a potential danger. They deserve confidentiality and the opportunity to change and even disappear.

A learning disability in itself is just a symptom. It is not the "disease." Until the "disease" and its root cause are defined, the treatment program remains vulnerable. de Hirsch's[44] statement seems much more appropriate, "In spite of such shortcomings, however, I feel that diagnosis is essential. The question is not diagnosis or no diagnosis, but *what kind* of diagnosis."

Interpret this statement simplistically. Keep the diagnostic labels simple, functional, appropriate, and provable; labels that all can understand, labels that lead to realistic therapeutic planning, particularly educational planning. Only then can children avoid the quagmire of the undocumented regimes mentioned above and others that continuously crop up.

An essential part of the total evaluation includes an assessment of parents' attitudes and their ability to understand and cope with the information presented to them. Maladaptive parental patterns should be considered secondary to the child's disability, rather than a causative factor, until proven otherwise.

In presenting the diagnosis to parents, it must be complete and specific in terms of strengths and weaknesses, it must lead to a therapeutic program in school and home, and it must present a prognosis and its influential variables. When appropriate, the diagnosis should be presented to the child.[45] However, caution is necessary in order to emphasize positive strengths and not conjure up negative self-images.

In the North American society, one is judged innocent until proven guilty. The parents of patients deserve at least that much consideration. Society has been thoroughly ingrained with the philosophy that whatever is wrong with the child can be blamed on the parents. Feelings of guilt reside in most effected parents. Unfortunately, many professionals not only do not allay this guilt, but indeed, reinforce it by continuing to harbor the "parents' fault" theory — consciously or unconsciously.

Regardless of the diagnosis, it is at this point, the point of presentation of the results of the evaluation to the parents, that their fears must be put in perspective and their guilt dissipated. This is a crucial moment. When parents resist or reject the diagnosis or treatment plan, why does the hurt professional become defensive? It must be recognized that the parents may not yet be ready for the results of the evaluation. Indeed, when there is disagreement, they may be right and the evaluation wrong. The problems uncovered often last a lifetime or, at the very least, influence a lifetime. Therefore, when parents disbelieve or want another opinion, do not discredit them; help them shop in the ethical market place rather than leave them prey to the quacks and charlatans.

DIAGNOSTIC CATEGORIES

Essential to the evaluation process is a thorough knowledge of the specific diagnostic conditions, *labels* that one may uncover. Vague, ill-defined concepts of the various learning disabilities will not do. The most prevalent of these conditions are listed and discussed briefly. While multiple diagnoses often present together, many studies suffer from attempts at drawing valid conclusions from hopelessly mixed experimental groups. For the sake of clarity, the categories are kept relatively "pure."

Cultural Deprivation

Most would agree that lack of cultural stimulation, with or without poverty, plays havoc with a child's learning and behavior. This is, by far, the most prevalent etiology of learning disability in this country. But, do not be lulled into thinking that every poor child with a learning problem needs no further evaluation. He is heir to the same specific deficits as anyone else. Poverty may be only an aggravating factor. Kappelman et al.[46,47] defined not only the various factors of poverty, but also the peripheral, related factors that influence school and behavioral performance of children. The significance of combined organic and functional psychosocial disorders is stressed. Family educational levels and perinatal and social factors all contribute to intellectual and learning deficits, over and above poverty per se.

Borderline Intelligence and Mild Mental Retardation

There are children with IQs in the borderline to high-educable range reared in excellent environments that help mask their limited potential. It is only when they get to school that one becomes aware of their deficits. Gruenberg[48] questioned whether the demands of society lead to a definition of mental retardation that is too stringent. In his study, the frequency of mental retardation was shown to change dramatically with age. From a very low rate, considerably below 1 percent in the newborn period, mental retardatoin increased gradually through the preschool years, then precipitously through the school years to a peak at age fourteen of approximately 6 percent. More significant, however, is the even more precipitous drop of approximately 50 percent in the frequency rate of apparent mental retardation as the school years fade. This would indicate that the demands of school cannot be satisfied by a sizable segment of the population that can "pass" when out of school.

Slow Learner

Pasamanick and Knoblock[49-51] have long been stressing the concept of a *continuum* in reproductive casualty and subsequent functional development. Certainly, this continuum exists in intellectual and academic abilities. Those children at the lower end of the "normal" scale without any other definable or measurable defects experience academic failure, whether their minimal limitations are aggravated by disadvantage or ovedwhelming by the competition of bright, advantaged peers.

Why have school systems found it necessary to burden so many of these "slow learners" with pathological labels? Preceding generations were wiser in just calling them "a little slow" and teaching them at their own level. Children were spared the "voodoo" labels.

Furthermore, some of these children represent what de Hirsch[44] calls *neurophysiological lags* and Ilg and Ames[52] term *superior immatures.* It must be recognized that these children, mostly boys, need nothing more than time to mature and a delay in starting the educational process. Vigorous intervention is contra-indicated.

Minimal Brain Dysfunction (MBD)

The number of articles, books, and position papers,[41,53-57] etc., on MBD published by the various professional disciplines is tremendous, but only exceeded in number by those from lay groups. Rather than rehashing definitions and descriptions, highlights of certain concepts of MBD will be presented. Kinsbourne,[1] among others, feels that use of the term *MBD* has become so all-inclusive as to be harmful. Conceptually, however, the label has merit, if used appropriately.

MBD is an "organic" condition; it is physiologically based. It can present with any one or combination of the following symptoms, but can also be free of any one or combination of these following symptoms.

Hyperkinesis: lack of impulse control, behavioral lability, excessive movement, short attention span

Coordination deficits: "soft" signs, clumsy fine and gross motor functions

Academic deficits: any or all areas of learning skills

Language deficits: expressive and receptive language, speech, concept formation

Perceptual deficits: visual, auditory, integrative

Intellectual deficits: verbal, performance, global, scattered

While many of these symptoms most frequently represent MBD (organicity), any one or combination of these can be present in the absence of organic brain dysfunction and can be due to other factors. Therefore, every case of suspected MBD represents a unique montage of signs and symptoms and must be approached on an individual basis.

Once a diagnosis of MBD is made, the surface has barely been scratched. A most complete analysis of the child's various strengths and weaknesses, the short– and long-term significance of each sign and symptom, the potential sequelae, the prognosis and the factors that influence that prognosis, and an analysis of the available therapeutic alternatives must be made. All this must be transmitted to the parents and school in precise terms. If not, then every labeled MBD child, regardless of his individual combination of deficits and strengths is relegated to the same brain-injured class or other such program of every other MBD child.

The following examples may help clarify these issues: The combination of hyperactivity, lack of impulse control, and short attention span is often presented as the hallmark of, and indeed, synonymous with, MBD. Yet the four-year-old who, for the first time, develops these exact symptoms because of a catastrophic family episode is not minimal brain dysfunction. The seven-year-old who, for the first time, develops these exact symptoms because he is dyslexic is not labeled an MBD child. While other historical and physical evidence is beneficial in making an accurate diagnosis, the single most important factor in diagnosis is asking and answering this question: When did symptoms really start? The true hyperkinetic was most often hyperkinetic from the beginning, often even as a fetus. MBD children can be geniuses, they can be retarded; they can be athletic champions, they can be "klutzes"; they can be extremely hyperkinetic; they can even be hypokinetic, if their impulsivity is directed to one activity from which they can't be removed.

While the "klutz" may be socially stigmatized in the "little league years," his lack of coordination is meaningless later on, if his ego survives. His ego will not survive the overzealous athletic father or Kephart[31] devotee. It will survive if other masculine outdoor activities in which the child can succeed are offered as alternatives. The seven-year-old who can not skip may well become his college's valedictorian. The eight-year-old with the terrible handwriting may become a literary giant. A famous author was once hurt when his ten-year-old son told him that he was a poor writer. Taken back, the author sheepishly attempted to defend himself by reeling off a long list of literary accomplishments. His son replied that he knew all that, but still could not decipher his father's handwriting.

Rosenbloom[58] states "Learning disabilities is not synonymous with MBD." There are many MBD children who are splendid students, who are not now, and never will be, poor students, and should not be tampered with in the early years, just because they demonstrate some equivocal signs suggestive of MBD. Obviously, the corollary is also true. There are many learning disabled who are not classified minimal brain dysfunction. Because they may also develop hyperactivity when they taste failure does not mean they go on stimulant therapy. The dyslexic or "slow learner" with secondary hyperactivity will not respond to, and indeed, may get worse on medication, in contradistinction to the true hyperkinetic.

Probably, the most significant functional manifestation of MBD in terms of prognosis (assuming intelligence is intact) and the need for amelioration is language impairment. Communication function is essential for acquisition of basic concepts, ability to follow instruction, arithmetic concepts, and even ego.[44] Failure to correct the language deficit with a long-term, ongoing program will lead to progressive academic failure. Deviant language function can be recognized by the pediatrician and every other professional that treats the child. Ask and answer the question, "Is the child's ability to understand and/or express language less developed than other functional areas?" Although formal evaluation by the language pathologist is often indicated, an appreciation of a language disability per se is well within the province of the pediatrician.

Dyslexia

If there is controversy over the term *MBD,* there is total war over the meaning and even existence of the term *dyslexia.* Each "army" has had its period of ascendancy and decline. In many state and local school districts the word is verboten.[42] Kinsbourne[1] "never uses that term." However, a long and ever-increasing list of authorities do: To the author, the evidence is irrefutable.[59-64]

The term *dyslexia* has probably been resisted for these reasons:

1. Once the classification is accepted, it becomes the responsibility of the educational system to set up very expensive remedial programs.
2. The term, as it is understood, is counter to the vogue of artificial dissection of every conceivable learning task. If one could not attach a *visuo* or *audio* or *percept.,al* or *encode* or *discrimination* or *memory,* etc., well then, the term just did not exist.

Critchley,[59] Boder,[61] Ingram,[62] de Hirsch,[44] would all agree with the basic concept of this statement: A dyslexic child is one in whom there are no, or almost no signs of neurological, intellectual, environmental, or primary psychological pathology, who has had adequate pedagogic exposure, and still is unable to read or spell with the same degree of success that he experiences in other areas.   Various authors have applied modifying appendages, all meaning essentially the same and each emphasizing an important attribute: *specific, primary, familial,* or *developmental.*

To put it in its most graphic terms — and these are exactly the terms the author uses to explain his evaluation to the dyslexic child and his parents: "He is bright and has no neurological problem.   There is not a thing wrong with the boy except that he's a lousy reader and speller."   Period.   Obviously, this often requires amplification if there are subtle lags in other areas, and particularly, if the child has developed associated secondary learning, behavioral, and emotional problems.   But the graphic statement stands.   And it stands because it directs (in contradistinction to any compromise with its message) the therapeutic program to the heart of the problem — reading and spelling.   It rejects any attempt to primarily treat the eyes, or the perception, or the emotions, or the coordination, or the right, or the left, or anything else, but reading and spelling.

Indeed, if a poor reader has significant pathology in any of the functional areas listed above, most authorities would be very wary in calling him a dyslexic.   Better to label him as a *symptomatic* or *secondary* or *nonspecific reading disability.*   In all probability, he will have a much more global learning dysfunction than the true dyslexic.

In the understanding of dyslexia, there are a number of points that must be stressed:

1. Dyslexia occurs far more frequently in boys than in girls.
2. Most cases are associated with a strong family history, usually involving father, uncles, and/or brothers — regardless of type of dyslexia.
3. Dyslexia represents a specific, often isolated developmental lag of varying degrees.

The basic defect in dyslexia is in the audiovisual integration mechanism as described by Birch and his associates.[65-67] Reading involves the recognition of a symbol, the transmission of that symbol into a *phoneme* (sound), combining a group of symbols and phonemes into a *morpheme* (word), and the extraction of a *meaning* from a combination of morphemes. Spelling is the reverse process. These processes require many relatively independent mechanisms.[64] For clinical purposes, however, these can be appropriately classified into three categories: deficits in phonetic transmission, deficits in word gestalt recognition, or deficits in both.

Although various authors describe the three types of dyslexia in different terms, many have reached relatively similar conclusions independently. Thus, Boder's[61] *dysphonic,* Ingram and others'[62] *audiophonic* and Myklebust's[68] *audio* forms of dyslexia are strikingly similar. This is, by far, the most common type and basically involves phonetic analysis deficits. Boder's *dyseidetic,* Ingram's *visuospacial* and Myklebust's *visual* essentially describe the same word gestalt recognition defect. Most severe are those dyslexics who have a combination of both types.

Boder[61] and Critchley[59] and others deemphasize the significance of other occasionally associated lags, findings, and types of errors as being part of the basic defect. Mild lags in right-left dominance and discrimination, coordination, perception, the disappearance of reversals and rotations, language development, and the tendency to lose one's place, omit and substitute letters, words, and punctuation, can be classified as, what Critchley calls, "epiphenomena — significant when they occur, but not essential in any consideration as to pathogenesis or etiology." If this is the

case, as it seems to be, then why is so much time and energy
devoted to defining and measuring and treating neurological and
psychometric epiphenomena, what Boder calls the *indirect diagnostic approach?* Attention should be focused, rather, on a *direct
diagnostic approach,* that is, clinically analyzing the qualitative
errors in the basic functions of reading and spelling.

To overstate the case, does perception (as it can be measured)
have anything to do with reading? Probably not. Any number
of children who produce terrible Bender figures yet read very
well have been seen. Certainly, the innumerable perceptual
materials available for therapy have little to offer the dyslexic.[34-36]
Even more certainly, the eye has very little to do with reading,
assuming there is functional vision. The uselessness of eye exercises is apparent.[29,30] Clinical analysis, as described above, leads
to clinical therapy for the specific nature of the reading defect.
As in many learning disabilities, treatment should involve en-
hancing and increased utilization of strengths before approaching
the weaknesses.

If that said above is correct, that is, diagnosis of dyslexia
ultimately hinges on an evaluation of reading and spelling, can,
then, as Jansky and de Hirsch[69] and others claim, this diagnosis be
made before the preschool child is exposed to reading, spelling,
and phonics? Clearly, it must be recognized that all such attempts must be based on evaluation of epiphenomena alone and,
therefore, are open to judicious suspicion. Snyder and Mortimer
[70,71] state, "Early identification may unnecessarily label a child
and may produce a self-fulfilling prophesy."

Psychogenic Learning Disability

Emotional disturbance and behavioral maladjustment are
viewed through prejudicial professional eyes. The spectrum of
opinion ranges from totally psychoanalytic to totally organic
predispositions.

Obviously, children who are significantly emotionally upset or
psychotic will most likely have severe learning disabilities, although there are some bright ambulatory schizophrenics who may
function and learn for sufficient periods of time to do well

academically.   Children with early unstable and inadequate mothering, who subsequently develop psychopathic personalities may also have difficulty learning, but some can do quite well. They may not be handicapped by an inhibiting superego that could stand in their way of success.   Clearly, severe and malignant emotional pathology in parents or their marriage and catastrophic disruptions in a family can create significant psychopathology and thus, learning disability in the child.   Such a history must be carefully sought in any evaluation.

One must question how much influence the usual, minor "neurotic" parental characteristics many of us possess or the usual day-to-day traumas have on an otherwise intact, well-endowed nervous system's ability to learn.   I submit that the majority of childhood psychogenic learning disorders are firmly based on a *substrate of subtle organic factors* that interfere with the attainment of a successful experience in some functional area.   The aberrant perception of, and response to, this deficit and its resultant failures on the part of the child compounds the disorder. Finally, and most condemning, is the conscious or unconscious recognition on the part of family, school, and peers that something is not quite right, with the resultant loss of their positive, spontaneous response toward the child.   Unless this is clearly recognized, psychotherapy, counseling, and play therapy, etc., are doomed to failure.   Again, a point is made with perhaps an overstated position: Unless the basic organic defects leading to failure in some area are recognized and ameliorated or compensated for, no amount or type of psychotherapy will help.   If this basic defect leading to failure can be replaced by positive, successful experience, then psychotherapy has a better chance to be beneficial or may not be necessary at all.

PRESCHOOL EVALUATION

Preschool evaluation is mentioned for the sake of completeness.   This is a complex topic in itself and deserves a total, separate discussion.   One must be extremely cautious in arriving at conclusions that may lead to "egg-on-the-face" in the future. As stated previously, many of the diagnostic tools available to us in the preschool period are potentially poor predictors of future academic achievement. This is not intended to mean that, when indicated, evaluation should be avoided. On the contrary, early evaluation is often essential. It is merely a word of caution.

ABSTRACT AND SUMMARY

This article defines the term *learning disability* and the role of the pediatrician in this disorder. The term represents an unexpected learning problem without any obvious intellectual, neurological, psycho-social, or pedagogical basis.

Controversial literature on the pediatric role is reviewed and eclectic conclusions drawn. There is a role for both primary pediatrician and pediatrician with special competence in normal and abnormal child development, including learning. Active pediatric participation may prevent further proliferation of undocumented diagnostic and therapeutic programs for learning-disabled and other handicapped children.

Inherent dangers and importance of *diagnostic labels* are discussed. The concept of parent as covictim of the disability rather than villain is stressed. Results and therapeutic implications of evaluations must be presented to parents in very specific terms.

Cultural deprivation, borderline and mild mental retardation, "slow learners," and psychogenic learning disorders are mentioned in the classification of learning disabilities. Definitions and highlights of, as well as distinctions between MBD and dyslexia are discussed. Prognostic and therapeutic implications of these "labels," as well as evidence to justify their use is presented. Pitfalls of overdiagnosis, particularly in the preschool period, are also treated.

REFERENCES

1. Kinsbourne, M.: School problems. *Pediatrics, 52:*697, 1973.
2. MacQueen, J.C.: Presidential address. Annual Meeting of the American Academy of Pediatrics, Washington, D.C., 1975.
3. Garrard, S.D.: Role of the pediatrician in the management of learning disorders. *Pediatr Clin North Am, 20:*737, 1973.
4. Kenny, T.J. and Clemmens, R.L.: Medical and psychological correlates

in children with learning disabilities. *J Pediatr, 78:*273, 1971.

5. Kenny, T.J., Clemmens, R.L., Cicci, R., Lentz, G.A., Nair, P., and Hudson, B.W.: The medical evaluation of children with reading problems (dyslexia). *Pediatrics, 49:*438, 1972.

6. Svoboda, W.B.: Reading disabilities, continued. *Pediatrics, 50:*969, 1972.

7. Snyder, R.D.: How much medical evaluation for reading disability? *Pediatrics, 50:*338, 1972.

8. Faigel, H.C.: How much medical evaluation for reading disability? *Pediatrics, 50:*339, 1972.

9. Schour, M. and Clemmens, R.L.: Fate of recommendations for children with school-related problems following interdisciplinary evaluation. *J Pediatr, 84:*903, 1974.

10. Committee on Children with Handicaps: *The Pediatrician and the Child with Mental Retardation.* Evanston, Illinois, The American Academy of Pediatrics, 1971.

11. Menkes, J.H.: A new role for the school physician. *Pediatrics, 49:*803, 1972.

12. Asbed, R., Fox, M.A., and Wender, E.: A new role for the school physician: Approval by those concerned. *Pediatrics, 50:*307, 1972.

13. Brown, G.W.: The school physician. *Pediatrics, 50:*149, 1972.

14. Frothingham, T.E.: The school physician. *Pediatrics, 50:*150, 1972.

15. Wassel, M.A.: The school physician and his role: A constructive conclusion. *Pediatrics, 50:*151, 1972.

16. Swaiman, K.: Presidential address. The Second Annual Meeting of The Child Neurology Society. Nashville, 1973.

17. Chamberlin, R.W.: New knowledge in early child development. *Am J Dis Child, 126:*585, 1973.

18. Brody, J.E.: Two doctors offer dyslexia theory. *The New York Times,* April 29, 1974.

19. Frank, J. and Levinson, H.: Dysmetric dyslexia and dyspraxia. Hypothesis and study. *J Am Acad Child Psychiatry, 12:*690, 1973.

20. Delacato, C.H.: *The Treatment and Prevention of Reading Problems.* Springfield, Thomas, 1959.

21. Doman, R.J., Spitz, E.B., Zuchman, E., Delacato, C.H., and Doman, G.: Children with severe brain injuries. Neurologic organization in terms of mobility. *JAMA, 174:*257, 1960.

22. Cohen, H.J., Birch, H.G., and Taft, L.T.: Some considerations for evaluating the Dorman-Delacato "patterning" method. *Pediatrics, 45:* 302, 1970.

23. Freeman, R.D.: Controversy over "patterning" as a treatment for brain damage in children. *JAMA, 202:*83, 1967.

24. Robbins, M.P.: Test of the Doman-Delacato rationale with retarded readers. *JAMA, 202:*87, 1967.

25. American Academy of Pediatrics: *Executive Board Statement, Am Acad*

Pediatr Newsletter, 16:1, 1965.

26. American Academy for Cerebral Palsy: *Statement of Executive Committee,* February 15, 1965.

27. Flax, N.: The eye and learning disabilities. *J Am Optometric Assoc, 43*:6, 1972.

28. Flax, N.: Visual function in learning disabilities. *J Learn Disabil, 1*:551, 1968.

29. Joint Organizational Statement: The eye and learning disabilities. *Am Acad Pediatr 49*:454, 1972.

30. *Report of the International Seminar on the Role of the Ophthalmologist in Dyslexia.* Dayton, Ohio, Institute for the Development of Education Activities, Inc., 1969.

31. Kepart, N.: *The Slow Learner in the Classroom.* Columbus, Ohio, Merrill, 1960.

32. Barsch, R.H.: *Achieving Perceptual—Motor Efficiency.* Seattle, Washington, Special Child Publications, 1967.

33. Frostig, M. and Horne, D.: *The Frostig Program for the Development of Visual Perception.* Chicago, Follett, 1964.

34. Church, M.: Does visual perception training help beginning readers? *The Reading Teacher,* Jan.: 361, 1964.

35. Bishop, J.S.: An investigation of the efficacy of the Frostig program for the development of visual perception. *Pediatrics, 50*:154, 1972.

36. Pitcher-Baker, G.: Does perceptual training improve reading? *Acad Ther, 9*:41, 1973.

37. Feingold, B.F.: *Why Your Child is Hyperactive.* New York, Random House, 1975.

38. Cott, A.: Orthomolecular treatment. A biological approach to treatment of schizophrenia. New York, *Am Schizophrenia Assoc,* 1970.

39. Schnackenberg, R.C.: Caffeine as a substitute for schedule II stimulants in hyperkinetic children. *Am J Psychiatry, 130*:796, 1973.

40. Pfeiffer, C.C., Sohler, A., Jenny, C.H., and Iliev, V.: Treatment of pyroluric schizophrenia (malveria) with large doses of pyridoxine and a dietary supplement of zinc. *J Orthomolecular Psychiatry, 3*:292, 1974.

41. Grossman, H.J.: *Current Management of Hyperactivity.* Presented at The American Academy of Pediatrics Annual Meeting, Washington, D.C., 1975.

42. *Special Education Rules and Regulations Pursuant to Title 18A, Chapter 46, New Jersey Administrative Code.* Division of Curriculum and Instruction, Branch of Special Education and Pupil Personnel Services. June, 1973.

43. Bateman, B.D.: Educational implications of minimal brain dysfunction. In de la Cruz, F.F., Fox, B.H., and Roberts, R.H. (Eds.): *Minimal*

Brain Dysfunction. New York, NY Academy of Science, 1973, p. 245-250.

44. de Hirsch, K.: Learning disabilities: An overview. *Bull NY Acad Med, 50:*459, 1974.

45. Gardner, R.A.: *The Child's Book About Brain Injury.* New York, Association for Brain Injured Children, 1966.

46. Kappelman, M.M., Luck, E., and Ganter, R.L.: Profile of the disadvantaged child with learning disorders. *Am J Dis Child, 121:*371, 1971.

47. Kappelman, M.M., Rosenstein, A.B. and Ganter, R.L.: Comparison of disadvantaged children, with learning disabilities and their successful peer group. *Am J Dis Child, 124:*875, 1972.

48. Gruenberg, E.M.: Epidemiology. In Stevens and Heber (Eds.): *Mental Retardation,* Chicago, U of Chicago Pr, 1964, p. 259.

49. Pasamanick, B. and Knoblock, H.: Retrospective studies on the epidemiology of reproductive casualty: Old and new. *Merril-Palmer Q Behav Dev, 12:*7, 1966.

50. Pasamanick, B. and Knoblock, H.: Prospective studies on the epidemiology of reproductive casualty: Methods, findings, and some implications. *Merril-Palmer Q Behav Dev, 12:*27, 1966.

51. Knoblock, H. and Pasamanick, B.: *Gesell and Amatruda's Developmental Diagnosis.* Hagerstown, Maryland, Har–Row, 1974.

52. Ilg, F. and Ames, L.: *School Readiness.* New York, Harper–Row, 1964.

53. de la Cruz, F., Fox, B.H., and Roberts, R.H. (Eds.): *Minimal Brain Dysfunction.* New York, New York Academy of Sciences, 1973.

54. Wender, P.H.: *Minimal Brain Dysfunction in Children.* New York, Wiley, 1971.

55. Eisenberg, L.: III. The clinical use of stimulant drugs in children. *Pediatrics, 49:*709, 1972.

56. Denhoff, E. and Tarnopol, L.: Medical responsibilities in learning disorders. In Tarnopol, L. (Ed.): *Learning Disorders in Children.* Boston, Little, 1971, p. 65.

57. Levine, M. (ed.): The hyperkinetic syndrome and minimal brain dysfunction. *Ann Pediatr, 25:* 1973.

58. Rosenbloom, L.: Learning disabilities and hyperkinesis. *Dev Med Child Neurol, 14:*394, 1972.

59. Critchley, M.: *The Dyslexic Child.* Springfield, Thomas, 1970.

60. Money, J. (Ed.): *Reading disability: Progress and Research Needs in Dyslexia.* Baltimore, Johns Hopkins, 1962.

61. Boder, E.: Developmental dyslexia: A diagnostic approach based on three atypical reading-spelling patterns. *Dev Med Child Neurol, 15:* 663, 1973.

62. Ingram, T.T.S., Mason, A.W., and Blackburn, I.: A retrospective study

of 82 children with reading disability.   *Dev Med Child Neurol, 12:* 271, 1970.

63. Naidoo, S.:   Symposium on reading disability 4.   Specific developmental dyslexia.   *Br J Educ Psychol, 41:*19, 1971.

64. Klassen, E.:   *The Syndrome of Specific Dyslexia.*   Baltimore, Univ Park, 1972.

65. Birch, H.G.:   *Brain Damage in Children.*   Baltimore, Williams & Wilkins, 1964.

66. Birch, H.G. and Belmont, L.:   Auditory–visual integration, intelligence and reading ability in school children.   *Percept Mot Skills, 20:*295, 1965.

67. Belmont, I., Birch, H.G. and Karp, E.:   The disordering of intersensory and intrasensory integration by brain damage.   *J Nerv Ment Dis, 141:* 410, 1966.

68. Myklebust, H.R.:   *Development and Disorders of Written Language.* New York, Grune, 1965.

69. Jansky, J. and de Hirsch, K.:   *Predicting Reading Failure.*   New York, Har–Row, 1972.

70. Snyder, R. D. and Mortimer, J.:   Dyslexia.   *Pediatrics, 44:*601, 1969.

71. Snyder, R.D. and Mortimer, J.:   Dyslexia.   *Pediatrics, 45:*344, 1970.

CHAPTER 4.

GENETICS AND THE HANDICAPPED CHILD

Jessica G. Davis, M.D.

RECENT advances in human genetics and medicine have in-creased the understanding of genetic disorders and permitted intelligent management of many resulting problems. An in-creased capacity to participate actively in reproductive decision making and behavior now exists. The chemical structure of DNA and the underlying biochemical mechanism for many hereditary disorders is understood. Tissue culture techniques permit labora-tory growth of cells and their biochemical and cytogenetic analysis. Many genetic disorders resulting in birth defects are amenable to surgical correction. Specific chromosome abnormali-ties, many inborn errors of metabolism, and some birth defects can now be accurately detected *in utero* with little risk to the mother or fetus. Genetic counseling services have expanded. There is also increased ability to detect genetic defects in asymp-tomatic carriers of mutant genes. Genetic screening programs have been implemented in many communities, resulting in a gradually increasing public awareness of problems of heredity. This cumulative increase in theory and practical application constitutes a quantum leap in knowledge.

In order to weigh such issues and to recognize the potential good as well as the inherent dangers in medical genetic advances, it is important to have some understanding of basic genetic prin-ciples and how genetic knowledge is applied today in medical practice.

A REVIEW OF CURRENT MEDICAL GENETIC PRINCIPLES

There are three major groups of genetic disorders: chromo-some disorders, mendelian (single gene) disorders, and multifactorial (polygenic) disorders.

The cells of all living organisms contain a fixed amount of genetic material in their nuclei. The genetic material is arranged in distinct units called *chromosomes*. Each chromosome is believed to contain hundreds, if not thousands, of *genes*. In humans most cells contain forty-six chromosomes or twenty-three like (homologous) pairs of chromosomes. Important exceptions are the reproductive cells, the ovum and the sperm, which each contain twenty-three unpaired chromosomes or one-half the number allotted to humans.

Of the twenty-three chromosome pairs, twenty-two pairs are termed *autosomes*. The remaining pair are called *sex chromosomes* and are identified as the X and the Y chromosomes. A normal human female is designated 46,XX because her total chromosomal number is 46, consisting of forty-four autosomes and two X chromosomes. A normal male is designated 46,XY because in addition to forty-four autosomes, males possess a single X chromosome and a single Y chromosome.

Chromosomal analysis is usually performed on special preparations of peripheral blood leukocytes. Similar studies can also be done on cells derived from bone marrow, skin biopsy, and amniotic fluid. The recent development of fluorescent staining or banding techniques enables precise chromosome identification and permits analysis of smaller chromosomal segments. Chromosomes are counted and arranged in pairs according to size, shape, and banding patterns. Each pair is then numbered according to a uniform system of identification.[1]

In 1959, Lejeune and his coworkers found an extra chromosome, 21, in white blood cells obtained from individuals with Down's syndrome or mongolism.[2] Affected individuals were said to have trisomy 21 or 47,XY+21 or 47,XX+21. This was the first time a specific chromosomal anomaly was linked to a constellation of clinical findings. Other human chromosome abnormality syndromes were reported, usually associated with either a structural rearrangement of chromosomal material or a deviation in the number of sex chromosomes or autosomes. The initial discoveries were made in persons exhibiting problems of sexual differentiation, physical malformations, mental retardation, or chronic myelogenous leukemia. Subsequently, gross chromosomal deviations have been found through laboratory studies on cells obtained from patients showing no evidence of physical or cognitive problems.

Chromosome disorders are classified as genetic, because there is either excessive or deficient chromosomal DNA. Cytogenetic abnormalities are seldom familial or inherited and usually occur as isolated events in single family's history. Chromosomal surveys of liveborn infants show that approximately 1 in 200 newborns displays a major chromosomal variation. The most frequently seen chromosome disorder is trisomy 21 in Down's syndrome with an overall frequency of 1 in 600 live births.

More than 2336 mendelian (single-gene) disorders have been described but the frequency of many of these clinical entities is presently unknown.[3] Single-gene disorders follow the classic patterns of inheritance established by Gregor Mendel in 1865.[4] They are classified according to their mode of genetic transmission as autosomal dominant, autosomal recessive, or X-linked recessive.

Mendelian disorders occur because of the presence and action of one or both of a pair of mutant genes. In order to understand Mendelian patterns of inheritance, it is important to know that genes encoding specific biochemical information occur in pairs and are located at specific chromosomal sites, or *loci*. Normal individuals receive one member of each gene pair and one member of each chromosome pair from each of their parents. Since human beings possess homologous pairs of autosomal chromosomes, each individual will have a pair of genes each situated at a given locus, one on each chromosomal homologue.

Genes can also occur at the same locus in alternative forms named *alleles*. Any given individual may have two alleles for a given unique but paired locus.[5] If this occurs, the protein products at such paired loci may not be identical. The term *nonallele* refers to genes at different loci. For example, the hemoglobin molecule is composed of two distinct biochemical subunits, alpha and beta chains. The genes for the α-chains of globin are nonalleles of the genes coding for the β-chains because there are two sets of gene pairs each located at different chromosomal sites.

Autosomal dominant disorders arise through mutation and are determined by genes that express themselves in a single dose in the male or female. Affected individuals have a mutant allele on one chromosome and a normal allele on the homologous chromosome at the identical locus. If a given autosomal dominant condition is not lethal and does not interfere with reproduction, the mutant autosomal dominant gene can be passed directly from one generation to the other. It is estimated that an affected individual with a known autosomal dominant condition has a 50 percent chance of transmitting the mutant gene to each of their offspring.

There are 1218 known autosomal dominant disorders.[3] Specific examples include primary hyperlipidemia and Huntington's disease. Five groups of disorders involving elevated plasma lipids have been identified and may affect 1 percent of the general population.[7,8] Findings include elevated plasma lipids and a predisposition of affected individuals to premature arteriosclerosis.[9] Evidence of type II disease, familial hyperbetalipoproteinemia can be obtained by testing one or more first-degree relatives. Affected individuals are now treated with appropriate drugs and dietary control of fat intake. At present there is no mechanism to identify all individuals at risk for this condition. Furthermore, little information exists about the efficacy of the therapeutic regimens in the prevention of vascular disease.[10-12]

Huntington's disease is a progressive lethal neurologic disorder. Affected individuals are usually diagnosed between the ages of thirty to forty years.[13] Cardinal features include dementia and chorea and rapid, writhing movements of the limbs, trunk, and face. The underlying biochemical defect is not known, and there is no specific diagnostic test available. A positive family history helps determine which individuals might develop Huntington's chorea, but usually the diagnosis can only be made when the clinical manifestations appear. There is also no satisfactory treatment for this disease. The incidence of this disorder in Michigan was reported as 1 in 25,000.[13]

Autosomal recessive disorders occur when both alleles in a particular gene pair are deleterious. Mutation gives rise to gene variants that often are transmitted through successive generations in the benign heterozygous or carrier state. However, if two clinically normal carriers of the same harmful gene mate, there is a 25 percent chance that their offspring will receive a double dose of the harmful genes and exhibit the characteristic symptoms of that particular autosomal recessive disorder. Statistically, such a carrier couple has the same 25 percent chance of giving birth to a child with a recessive disorder with each pregnancy.

As of January, 1976, investigators have identified 947 autosomal recessive disorders, including Tay-Sachs disease and many inborn errors of metabolism.[3] Tay-Sachs disease is a disorder of sphingolipid storage associated with a deficiency of an enzyme, hexosaminidase A in the brain, blood, and other tissues.[14] The lack of enzyme results in the accumulation of GM_2 ganglioside in the cells of the central nervous system. Neurological symptoms first appear in infants of about six months of age and progress, resulting in death at four to six years. There is no treatment for Tay-Sachs disease. It occurs primarily in the offspring of Jews of Eastern European origin with a frequency of approximately 1 in 3000 live births.[15] Sensitive, reliable tests identify the affected homozygote, as well as the heterozygote or carrier.[6]

Phenylketonuria (PKU) is another example of an inborn error of metabolism. Individuals with PKU lack adequate phenylalanine hydroxylase, an enzyme which is necessary for the metabolism of phenylalanine. Severe and irreversible developmental deterioration occurs if an affected individual is not diagnosed and treated shortly after birth.[17] Most states have adopted inexpensive, simple, and accurate compulsory measures to screen for PKU in the newborn period.[18] Treatment consists of instituting a low-phenylalanine diet shortly after birth. The diet is effective in preventing a substantial amount of the otherwise inevitable mental retardation.

The X-linked recessive disorders occur primarily in males and are transmitted by females. Males have a single X chromosome and a single Y chromosome. The Y chromosome (only) bears the gene or genes necessary for differentiation of the testes. Males have a single copy of the genes on the X chromosome. If a male's X chromosome contains a harmful allele, he will have an X-linked recessive disorder, such as hemophilia A or Duchenne type muscular dystrophy. Females are usually heterozygous for X-linked recessive genes and are generally aysmptomatic. Females become carriers of X-linked recessive disorders either by inheriting the gene from their mothers or through a fresh mutation.

Recurrence risks can be accurately calculated for X-linked recessive disorders. The sex chromosome makeup of a male is determined by the fact that he inherits an X chromosome from his mother and a Y chromosome from his father. Similarly, a female with an XX sex chromosome complement receives one X from her mother and one X from her father. Thus, there is a 50 percent chance of having either a girl or a boy with each pregnancy. If the mother's X chromosomes are free of aberrant X-linked recessive alleles, she has a 50 percent chance of having a normal male infant and a 50 percent chance of having a normal female child because she transmits only normal X chromosomes. However, if she is a carrier of an X-linked recessive disorder she still has a 50 percent chance of having a son; of her sons, 50 percent are at risk for having an X-linked disorder and 50 percent will be problem-free. Although all of her daughters would be normal, 50 percent run the risk of being carriers of an X-linked recessive allele like their mother, and the remaining 50 percent would not be carriers.

Approximately 150 X-linked recessive disorders have been identified.[3] One of the most common is a deficiency of a red blood cell enzyme, glucose-6-phosphate dehydrogenase (G-6-PD).[19] Many molecular variants of human G-6-PD have been identified. For instance, the A variant associated with G-6-PD deficiency is found in approximately 10 to 14 percent of black males in the United States. Mild hemolysis or a breakdown of red blood cells will occur if affected individuals are exposed to oxidant drugs, such as antimalarials. Hemophilia A is another X-linked recessive disorder characterized by a coagulation defect caused by a marked reduction of plasma factor VIII activity. The frequency of severe hemophilia A is estimated at 1 in 8600 males.[20] Recent technological advances have made prophylactic therapy possible. However, supplies of concentrate are too limited for a continuing program of prophylactic treatment of a large, affected population.[21] Currently, hemorrhagic episodes are managed with concentrates of factor VIII, fresh-frozen plasma, or lyophilized plasma.

Polygenic or multifactorial problems constitute the third group of genetic disorders. It is believed that polygenic disorders result from the interaction of many gene pairs with each other and with environmental factors. This diagnostic category includes many congenital malformations, such as cleft lip, cleft palate, clubfoot, and defects of the developing neural tube. The true incidence of polygenic disorders is unknown. Statistical evidence varies because of differences in the ages of the study sample, diagnostic criteria, methods of ascertainment, and skills of the observers. In an Edinburgh study of 8684 babies, 5.4 percent had congenital malformations, with major abnormalities occurring in 2.1 percent and minor abnormalities in 3.3 percent.[22] A Swedish study of 6200 infants showed 3.3 percent had major anomalies and 9.6 percent exhibited minor problems.[23]

The probability of recurrence for most polygenic disorders is low. More accurate recurrence risk figures can be calculated for certain polygenically inherited disorders, such as spina bifida, depending on the exact family history and the number of previously affected offspring.

Individuals and families seek genetic services for many reasons. Some have given birth to a child with a genetic disorder or a congenital malformation. Others have clinical evidence of a genetic problem or have an affected family member. Women who are thirty-five and older should seek genetic information, because they are at greatly increased risk for giving birth to a child with a chromosome anomaly. Some couples wish to discuss problems associated with consanguinity. Many women are worried about the effects of exposure to potential or actual environmental hazards upon the outcome of pregnancy and also upon their own genetic material. Others may have a history of miscarriages.

Many individuals come because of problems with growth and with the development of secondary sex characteristics. Some persons come for carrier detection tests.

The number of individuals seeking genetic services increases each year. There has also been an increase in the total number of genetic units so that there are now more than 600 genetic programs in the United States. All of the genetic programs are hospital-related programs with associated laboratory services. Some major medical centers have developed satellite clinics to reach out into surrounding communities and to remote geographic areas. Genetic services are delivered by a multidisciplinary team made up of medical geneticists, physicians, nurses, social workers, associates in genetic counseling, laboratory personnel, and office staff.

The genetic counseling process begins with determining the reasons for and source of the referral. If an individual or family has no knowledge of genetics, time must be spent outlining the scope of the program. Individuals and families should understand that before they can be advised of their actual risks and options, all aspects of the problem must be fully explored.

The counselor then obtains a complete family history and draws up a detailed pedigree. All past and present medical problems are reviewed systematically. The history includes data about the individual's age, nationality, habits, diet, hobbies, education, and vocation. Possible exposure of the patient to infection and environmental hazards such as x rays, drugs, and chemicals is investigated. If pertinent, the counselor reviews the facts concerning conception, spontaneous abortion, stillbirths, and method of contraception. The counselor will study all available records, including medical, birth, and autopsy reports. Examination of family records and photographs may prove helpful.

The affected individual and possibly other close relatives then undergo a complete physical examination. If necessary, medical consultation is obtained from such specialists as neuro–, ophthalmo–, and audiologists. Specific laboratory tests, including biochemical and cytogenetic studies, are performed. When the information gathering is complete, the genetic counselor reviews all the assembled data, including the results of any laboratory tests and tries to arrive at a precise diagnosis. The counselor first decides whether the problem is genetic or is caused by a known environmental factor. If environmental factors are ruled out, the counselor attempts to pinpoint the mode of inheritance.

Next, the counselor outlines his conclusions to the concerned individual or family at an informing interview. At this time the counselor reviews the reasons for referral and the history, the pertinent findings of physical examination, and the laboratory data. Discussion focuses on the diagnosis and the prognosis or what to expect in the future. The mode of inheritance and the recurrence risks are fully explained. Lastly, all possible options are considered, such as appropriate therapeutic measures or amniocentesis.

Genetic counseling is time consuming. Counselors and their patients need time to exchange information and to absorb all the facts. Additional follow-up sessions may be necessary in order to answer questions and to more thoroughly communicate genetic concepts. Many counselors send detailed letters to their patients summarizing the results of the genetic work-up.

What is the effect on individuals who have gone through genetic counseling or even a group screening? Will they avoid conception at all costs? Will they accept low risks of conceiving children with genetic problems? Will their sex life be thrown off kilter? Unfortunately, genetic counselors have barely begun to ask these questions, and the answers are far from definitive.

Carter et al. examined the response of 455 couples to a variety of genetic disorders and to counseling.[24] All of the couples had been seen in their genetics unit three to ten years earlier. Their results showed that parents of patients with a high risk of repetition and high morbidity and mortality were generally deterred from further reproduction. Parents of patients with less severe handicapping conditions and a high or low risk of recurrence did not curtail reproduction. Their follow-up study also revealed that most parents understood the nature of the disorder and their risks.

Less optimistic results were reported by Leonard, Chase, and

Childs.[25] Their study was designed to study the attitudes of parents toward genetic counseling and the reasons for its success or failure. They reported on the reactions of parents with children with known genetic diseases who had received genetic counseling, as well as on parents of children with severe nongenetic disorders who had not received counseling. Evidence given by these families suggests that reproductive attitudes are determined more by the sense of burden imparted by the disease than by knowledge of its precise risk figures.

The term *burden* refers to the medical problems of the disease, including early mortality, as well as the parents' perceptions of the physical, emotional, and financial load. Of the families counseled, 50 percent had a good grasp of the information, 25 percent gained some knowledge, and 25 percent learned very little. The authors found that the obstacles to effective genetic counseling include lack of public awareness, limited knowledge of human biology and genetics; and differences in the contexts in which the counseling was provided, as well as the personal qualities, ability to communicate, and knowledge of the physicians providing the information.

More information is needed about technique and results of genetic counseling. Investigations on the effect of genetic counseling on larger populations and for a variety of medical disorders has not been done. The complexity of the role genetic counseling plays in decision making for common multifactorial problems remains untouched. More data are needed on the factors that motivate persons to seek or avoid genetic counseling.

REFERENCES

1. Hamerton, J.L., Jacobs, P.A., and Klinger, H.P. (Eds.): Standardization in human cytogenetics. *Birth Defects, 8,7:* 1972.
2. Lejeune, J., Gautier, M., and Turpin, R.: Les chromosomes humains en culture de tissus. *C R Acad Sci (Paris), 248:*602, 1959.
3. McKusick, V.A.: *Mendelian Inheritance in Man: Catalogs of Autosomal Dominant, Autosomal Recessive and X-linked Phenotypes,* 4th ed. Baltimore, Johns Hopkins, 1975, pp. lviii-lxviii.
4. Mendel, Gregor: Experiments in plant hybridization. In Peters, J.A. (Ed.): *Classic Papers in Genetics.* Englewood Cliffs, P-H, 1959, pp. 1-20.

5. Harris, H.: *The Principles of Human Biochemical Genetics,* 2nd ed. New York, Am Elsevier, 1975, pp. 278-367.

6. Fredrickson, D.S. and Lees, R.S.: A system for phenotyping hyperlipoproteinemia. *Circulation, 31:*231, 1965.

7. Glueck, C.J. et al.: Neonatal familial type II hyperlipoproteinemia: Cord blood cholesterol in 1800 births. *Metabolism, 6:*597, 1971.

8. Goldstein, J.L. et al.: Hyperlipidemia in coronary heart disease. I. Lipid levels in 500 survivors of myocardial infarction. II. Genetic analysis of lipid levels in 176 families and delineation of a new inherited disorder, combined hyperlipidemia. III. Evaluation of lipoprotein phenotypes of 156 genetically defined survivors of myocardial infarction. *J Clin Invest, 52:*1533, 1544, 1569, 1973.

9. Kennel, W.B., Castelli, W.P., Gordon, T., and McNamara, P.M.: Serum cholesterol, lipoproteins and the risk of coronary heart disease. *Ann Intern Med, 74:*1, 1971.

10. Task Force on Arteriosclerosis: *Arteriosclerosis.* National Heart and Lung Institute, June, 1971.

11. Glueck, C.J. and Tsang, R.C.: Pediatric familial type II hyperlipoproteinemia: Effects of diet on plasma cholesterol in the first year of life. *Am J Clin Nutr, 25:*224, 1972.

12. Kennel, W.B. and Dawber, T.R.: Arteriosclerosis as a pediatric problem. *J Pediatr, 80:*544, 1972.

13. Chandler, J.H., Reed, T.E., and Dejong, R.N.: Huntington's chorea in Michigan. *Neurology, 10:*148-153, 1960.

14. Okada, S. and O'Brien, J.S.: Tay-Sachs disease: Generalized absence of a beta-d-n-acetylhexosaminidase component. *Science, 165:*698-700, 1969.

15. Aronson, S.M.: Epidemiology. In Volk, B.W. (Ed.): *Tay-Sachs Disease.* New York, Grune, 1964.

16. Brady, R.O., Johnson, W.G., and Uhlendorf, B.W.: Identification of heterozygous carriers of lipid storage diseases. *Am J Med, 51:*423, 1971.

17. Knox, W.E.: Phenylketonuria. In Stanbury, J.B., Wyngaarden, J.B., and Fredrickson, D.S. (Eds.): *The Metabolic Basis of Inherited Disease,* 3rd ed. New York, McGraw, 1972, pp. 266-295.

18. Guthrie, R. and Susi, A.: A simple phenylalanine method for detecting phenylketonuria in large populations of newborn infants. *Pediatrics, 32:*338, 1963.

19. Beutler, E.: Glucose-6-phosphate dehydrogenase deficiency. In Stanbury, J.B., Wyngaarden, J.B., and Fredrickson, D.S. (Eds.): *The Metabolic Basis of Inherited Disease,* 3rd ed. New York, McGraw, 1972, p. 1358.

20. Department of Health, Education and Welfare, Public Health Service, National Institutes of Health: *Summary Report: NHLI's Blood Resource Studies.* Publ. No. (NIH) 73-416; 1972, p. 101.

21. Meyers, R.D. et al.: The social and economic impact of hemophilia—A survey of 70 cases in Vermont and New Hampshire. *Am J Public Health, 62*:530, 1972.
22. Nelson, M.M. and Forfar, J.O.: Congenital abnormalities at birth: Their association in the same patient. *Dev Med Child Neurol, 11:* 3, 1969.
23. Ekelund, H., Kullander, S., and Kallen, B.: Major and minor malformations in newborns and infants up to one year of age. *Acta Paediatr Scand, 59*:297, 1970.
24. Carter, C.O. et al.: Genetic clinic: A follow-up. *Lancet, 1*:281, 1971.
25. Leonard, C.O., Chase, G.A., and Childs, B.: Genetic counseling: A consumer's view. *N Engl J Med, 287*:433-439, 1972.

CHAPTER 5.

THE VALUE OF RESOURCE ROOMS AND ITINERANT TEACHING: A PLACE ON THE CONTINUUM

PHOEBE LAZARUS, Ed.D.

THE DEVELOPMENT OF A CONTINUUM OF EDUCATIONAL SERVICES

As SPECIAL education entered the twentieth century, the need for alternatives to residential public or private schools had been voiced frequently; yet, service delivery was practiced in a rather prescribed way. For one-half century, special classes or special schools were the program placement most frequently observed. These practices were not confined to the moderately and maximally impaired alone. Categorically labeled minimally impaired learners also found themselves in segregated instructional settings; only a small percentage were maintained in regular classes.

The notion that supportive services could assist certain of the handicapped to stay in regular classes was an exception to this rule and was applied primarily to sensorially impaired students. It was only thirty years ago that itinerant teaching for visually handicapped and hearing handicapped children created a "breakthrough" as a successful alternative to special schools and special classes. This system of service delivery was not then available to children with other handicaps.

Midcentury special education had been represented by only levels 5, 6, 7, and 8 on the now familiar *cascade system of special education service* (Fig. 5-1). These levels would signify that instruction for school-age handicapped (physically handicapped, educable mentally retarded, and emotionally disturbed) was

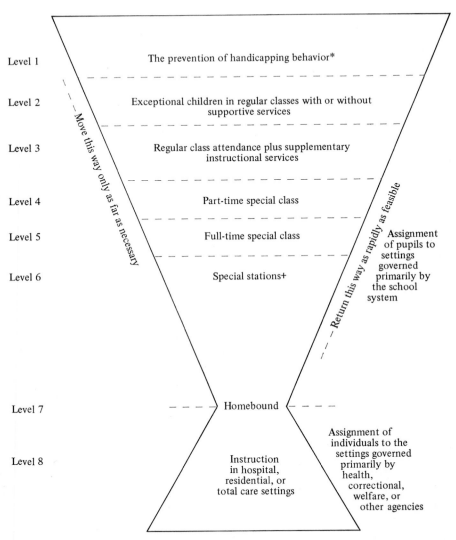

Level 1   The prevention of handicapping behavior*

Level 2   Exceptional children in regular classes with or without supportive services

Level 3   Regular class attendance plus supplementary instructional services

Level 4   Part-time special class

Level 5   Full-time special class

Level 6   Special stations+

Move this way only as far as necessary

Return this way as rapidly as feasible

Assignment of pupils to settings governed primarily by the school system

Level 7   Homebound

Level 8   Instruction in hospital, residential, or total care settings

Assignment of individuals to the settings governed primarily by health, correctional, welfare, or other agencies

* This means the development of positive cognitive, affective, and psychomotor skills in all pupils that will reduce or prevent the frequency of handicapping behavior.
+ Special schools in public school systems.

Figure 5-1. The cascade system of special education service. From Evelyn Deno, Special Education as Developmental Capital, *Exceptional Children,* *235,* 1970. Courtesy of The Council on Exceptional Children, Reston, Virginia.

rendered in totally restricted environments in the residential settings (level 8), home instruction (level 7), special schools (level 6), or special self-contained classrooms (level 5).

In New York State, itinerant teaching for other than sensorially impaired children was first attempted in 1960. The author was happily the first teacher, since she was the proposer of the notion, and one often is "volunteered" under such circumstances. The school district was Levittown, Long Island, and for the next three years, the principals, psychologists, and classroom and itinerant teachers studied the types of elementary school children who could benefit from such support services.

By today's definitions, the eighty-five children identified and served might be called *learning disabled*. Those who were successfully maintained in regular classes were of average or near average intelligence, minimally behaviorally disordered, minimally brain damaged, and minimally motor impaired. In a 1964 northeast regional Council for Exceptional Children (CEC) convention, a presentation was made describing a Levittown team cooperative effort that sustained a hearing-impaired, brain-injured boy in regular classes for two years. That same year, the noncategorical terminology of *learning disabilities* was beginning to stir the educators' and the parents' imagination. Increasingly, itinerant teaching was attempted.

Especially useful to small school districts and rural areas, *itinerant teachers, consultant teachers* and various traveling support instructors made a significant contribution to creating other options than self-contained special classes and "integrated" special classes whose members joined regular classes in nonacademic activities. Ohio and Michigan were among the many states that developed nationally recognized itinerant services for emotionally, neurologically and sensorially handicapped students.

By the late 1960s, mainstreaming was emerging as a strong force in public education. With it came the introduction of *resource teachers* in many flexible service-delivery options. Resource teachers frequently assumed roles of direct service to children, as well as indirect services as consultants to other school personnel. Titles of *itinerant, resource room, consultant, helping teacher, prescriptive teacher, psychoeducational diagnostician* and many other nomenclatures emerged in the personnel rosters. Learning centers to which children would come on a scheduled basis for specific skill area training increased as multimedia technology and computer-managed instruction also flourished.

Many influences brought about the evolution of mainstreaming. Among these forces were parent groups, civil rights movements, and tests of the law regarding provision of education and miscategorizing of minority-group students. Concurrent with the movements toward least restrictive environments were changes in the fields of psychological and educational theory. Developmental and cognitive psychology, plus the strong push toward individualization as an ideal strongly influenced special and regular education environments. The continuum of services for the handicapped was enriched by the development of upper cascade levels such as preventative developmental curricula (level 1); maintenance of children in regular classes with or without supportive services (level 2); regular class attendance plus supplementary instructive services (level 3); and part-time special classes with students integrated into regular classes for both academic and nonacademic subjects (level 4).

At this writing, resource rooms seem to be the most widely accepted supportive service format. They have demonstrated their flexibility with regard to student age, level, and type of educational need. Direct service may be supplied to fifteen to twenty children who need intensive individual intervention. In addition, the resource room provides an indirect service to many students through demonstration and consultation with regular classroom teachers.

A moment to look at public school support services for children's learning disabilities is in order. In general, any school system and its ancillary services is said to be supportive to administrators, teachers and students. Specifically, when preventive, developmental, ameliorative and remediative measures are considered, specialists tend to make up the "cadre" of support personnel.

School nurses, teachers, psychologists, guidance personnel, curriculum specialists, speech therapists, physical educators, music, art, and industrial arts teachers have always been considered special support people. Of late, new roles regarding learning disabilities are being developed around assessment and remediation by these specialists for "mainstreamed" children. Their roles are implemented either as individuals or members of a learning team.

The learning specialist on a learning team appears now to be either a regular classroom teacher with additional skills in diagnosis and remediation or a special educator in a changing role from a classroom to resource teacher. These roles relate to specific children, under the regular curriculum, whose needs have been found to be exceptional.

Paraprofessionals are often seen in assisting roles to a resource teacher or resource team. These persons may be undergraduate or graduate students in education, psychology, speech and language or reading, and, as such, are viewed as instructional support staff. Trained aides, often high-school graduates, are also seen as supporting the teacher under supervision. High school students in independent study at the high schools or earning community service credits are among the volunteers who appear to be most motivating and motivated in the resource room. Many resource teachers are also successfully guiding cross-age and peer "tutors," who are themselves resource room students or former resource room children.[8]

School programs have not always been creative and innovative. A great conversion has appeared in some buildings as a way of demonstrating to various public pressure groups that steps are being taken toward resource services.

In some schools, conversion has been merely a change in the sign on the classroom door. Libraries have been retitled *instructional media centers;* self-contained classrooms have been renamed *individualized instruction laboratories;* remediation centers for math and reading have been converted into distribution points for materials and machines processing children through assumedly individualized instruction. Some rooms are actually teacher-supervised tutoring centers with paraprofessionals and volunteers following packaged programs for deficit remediation. Finally, some rooms are operating solely on assessment of inefficiencies in learning with clinical teaching of specific deficits as the major approach in lieu of instruction in basic school subjects.

Classroom teachers are also receiving varied support in terms of inservice training. "Training" often consists of lectures by "experts" on the identification of specific learning disabilities. Most of these occur after school; occasionally summer inservice workshops include demonstration and actual "hands-on" experience with identified children.

The special education instruction media networks and regional resource centers are running teacher training and retraining inservice workshops. Films and multimedia kits are also being published to assist the local staffs of schools to develop "expertise."

Consensus does exist, however, on the major logistics of resource rooms. The arguments are rampant on whether they should focus on improving performance on school tasks, remediating prerequisite psychoeducational subskills, diagnosing interferences and developing prescriptions for regular class teachers to follow, or "engineered classroom" techniques.[4] Actually, a resource room might do any and all of these and *should* do so to effectively serve the varieties of students and the varieties of environmental components with which they are faced.

The quotation below is typical of accepted definitions in state education department regulations. It comes from the New York State definition (Section 209, 184 (200.1) f.)

> EXCERPTS: *Amendments to the Regulations of the Commissioner of Education Pursuant to Section 209 of the Education Law*

184 (200.1) *Definitions*

f. A "Resource Room" is a classroom area of adequate size to accommodate a special teacher, a small group of students as well as the specialized equipment necessary for instruction of handicapped children registered in special or regular classes who are in need of specialized supplementary instruction for varying periods during the day depending upon the severity of the handicapping condition and the educational needs of the child. Such a facility can be utilized as the foundation for a special educational program for handicapped children.*

*Education of Children with Handicapping Conditions, Regents' Position Paper No. 20 (1973).

THE LEARNER IN A RESOURCE ROOM

Since a resource room is by name and definition a room for special support, it is important to name and define the recipients of such support.

A supportive service does not replace special programs for severely handicapped learners. Children with severe handicaps who *can* learn in regular classes are included in mainstream situations. It is the severely handicapped person whose learning is also severely impaired that needs a special environment and for whom the resource room is inappropriate. Multiply handicapped and profoundly behaviorally disordered students are among those for whom this model may be unfeasible.

Those who can benefit from resource rooms are generally mildly to moderately handicapped children. It is not uncommon, therefore, to find socially adjusted educable mentally retarded students; children with minimal brain dysfunction; children with visual and auditory impairments; children with mild motor incoordination; and children with specific language disabilities scheduled individually or in groups of two to five children with similar educational needs.

While the earliest and fastest growth in resource programs has been for students in the elementary grades, recently, middle school, junior high school and senior high school programs have been increasing. The field reports on elementary school programs have been quite positive, and some favorable results are being reported in the literature and at national conventions since 1970.

The secondary level programs, however, are still under study. Student reaction to "pullout" systems is occasionally negative and resistant. In recognition of this factor, resource teams (teachers of various basic school subjects trained in remediative and compensatory teaching) seem to be appearing as a more accepted support than a remediation center at junior and senior high school levels.

DIMENSIONS TO BE CONSIDERED IN RESOURCE ROOM MODELS

It may be observed, in visiting or readings, that the focus of resource room services changes according to age level of students.

In the early grades (kindergarten through second grade), prevention of further deficit by developmental instruction is the major emphasis. In the intermediate grades, remediation is a very clearly seen emphasis. In middle schools, junior high schools and senior high schools, the swing is quite definite to compensatory training.[8]

Another dimension to be observed is in objectives set by the local school. One program may emphasize behavior change relative to attitudes, failure syndrome, dependency and impulse control. A second may emphasize increased efficiency through intensive short-term training in specific skill areas. A third focus is on supportive instruction (long-term training in multideficit areas such as attention, memory, and time and space concepts).

A third dimension relates to grouping. Some schools cling to intensive individual instruction. Others rarely operate with individuals and schedule groups of two to five children. Still others set up lower regular class registers (fifteen to twenty students) in an open-classroom style focused on specific individual deficits with a concern for the transfer of learning to the larger group.

Pitfalls and Clinkers

Great misunderstandings occur in schools initiating or operating resource rooms. Major misperceptions by administrators, psychologists, teachers, and parents relate to resource room or resource teacher function. Consider the following quotations as instances of this confusion:

Teacher: "I thought you were here to work on reading."
"Don't take him out during reading, math, phys. ed, science, social studies, or art and music (at which he is failing, by the way) because he'll miss something."
"Why aren't you taking Jimmy? He's driving me and the whole class up the wall."

Psychologist: "What prescription are you working on?" (it changes from day to day, or nothing is happening).

Parent: "Why aren't you teaching him to read?"
"When is he going to catch up with the others?"
"Why aren't his achievement scores higher now?"

Adminis- "How many more kids can we put into the resource
trator: room? You're only working with twenty. We have
thirty more who need help."

"When are you going to work in School B. You're
spending all your time in School A."

Even when the staff of a school and the parents are included
in initial planning and interpretations, misconceptions persist.
Any innovation "rocks the boat" and needs ongoing interpretation and reinforcement.

Teacher selection is another serious problem. Current eco-
nomics in the schools may find the administration selecting a
relatively inexperienced graduate from a new university program
in learning disabilities. Perhaps a teacher who might have been
excessed is "saved" by appointment as a resource room teacher.
Again, reading teachers, whose positions are threatened since they
are not classroom assigned, may be selected to perform as resource room teachers on the premise that all learning disabilities
are actually instances of reading disability and/or specific language disability. Special class teachers, whose students have been
"mainstreamed," are also candidates for the resource room role.
It is not inferred that any of the mentioned persons could not
perform admirably. What is intended is the serious consideration
of the skills necessary to perform as a resource teacher.

The consultant teacher facet of resource room teaching requires a special skill in nonthreatening diplomacy—a colleague-
ship posture of soft persuasion but obvious "know-how." Experienced regular class teachers working with an inexperienced but
"trained" learning disability resource teacher may discover that
their own grasp of systematic sequential instruction strands and
individualization skills may be at a higher developmental level
than the "specialist."

The teacher receiving consultant help needs to feel that the
person supporting him/her has at least equal skills in observing,
recording, and analyzing learning behavior and response error.
A skilled diagnostician and method tester is needed for effective
partnership in working with the classroom teacher.

The maker of profiles of test results and other information

about a student must also be competent in selecting relevant, achievable objectives for both short- and long-term intervention; in performing and demonstrating task analysis; in analyzing media for instruction toward an appropriate student-medium match; and in analyzing learner style toward selection of appropriate methods. Selection of the method must be considered in the light of feasibility in total group, small group, and one-to-one instructional conditions.

Keith Beery[1] pointed out some of the serious difficulties that can emerge when the school community has not reached its own accord on definitions and practices regarding resource rooms and resource teachers. Among the problems to be resolved are —

1. Shall classes for the handicapped be dissolved?
2. If resource rooms are opened or resource teachers employed, shall they work with all kinds of kids?
3. Does that include the gifted and the culturally different?
4. Should the youngest children be served on a priority basis?
5. How many children can be served by one teacher?
6. Who selects the children and how?
7. Who administers the program? Is it special education? General education? Conjoint operation?

FIELD REACTIONS TO RESOURCE ROOMS AND RESOURCE TEACHING

In Long Island, New York, with fifteen years of experience in support services for mainstreamed moderately to mildly impaired learners, reactions were recently requested by the writer from fifty resource teachers in thirty Nassau County school districts. They were asked for open comments on the pros and cons of "pullout systems" with the following results:

Pro: Intensive intervention can be provided by a resource teacher, and this offer gives the primary grade young child a "running start" on amelioration of specific language disabilities.

Con: Certain children, especially the middle school and older, perceive the "pullout" for one-to-one or small group instruction as stigmatizing and may reject help.

Pro: Clinical teaching techniques are possible in a resource room setting that are not feasible or accepted in a regular classroom environment. Moreover, the observation of these techniques is serving as formidable inservice training stimulation.

Con: Transition of skills learned in one-to-one relationship is frequently not adequate. Sometimes, this is because it takes special planning and team interaction with regular class teachers. Therefore, transfer of new learnings to a full setting is at risk.

Pro: Precision teaching can continue to get at ongoing problems in connection with specific short-term objectives.

Con: Identification of specific objectives and need for external support often tend to lower expectations by the regular class teacher.

Pro: School-based resource teachers can offer reality-based suggestions for pupil and instructional management backed up by their experience.

Con: Many regular class teachers tend to transfer responsibility for the education of the disabled child to the expert. This, in turn, reinforces feelings of inadequacy in the sending teacher.

Pro: When seen as a team-teaching alternative (a *shared* responsibility), support of the mainstreamed child is more effective, better organized, and more accepted. The team seems to know who does what to whom, how, when, and why.

The evaluation of resource services is only now beginning. All that has been recorded above is limited by the biases of the writer and her informants. One thing, however, is clear: The potential for effective support to both child and teacher and for enhancement of regular class teaching skills is formidable. A regular, special education teamwork is evolving, and, hopefully, new interactive roles will improve education for *all* children who have learning difficulties.

REFERENCES

1. Beery, K.: *The Guts to Grow.* San Rafael, California, Dimensions Publications, 1974.
2. Hammill, D.D. and Wiederholt, J.L.: *The Resource Room: Rationale and Implementation.* Fort Washington, Pennsylvania, J Spec Educ Pr, 1972.
3. Heller, H.W.: The resource room: A mere change or real opportunity for the handicapped. *J Special Educ, 6:*369-376, 1972.
4. Hewett, F.M.: Handicapped children and the regular classroom. In Reynolds, M.C., and Davis, M.D.: *Exceptional Children in Regular Classrooms.* U.S. Office of Education, 1968.
5. Jenkins, J.R. and Mayhall, W.P.: Development and evaluation of a resource training program. *Exceptional Children, 43, 1:*21-29, 1975.
6. Kandelakas, G.: Resource: A needed alternative. *Conveyor, 3,2:* 1-3, 1975. Board of Cooperative Educational Services, Putnam-Northern Westchester County, New York.
7. Lazarus, P.W.: *Itinerant Teaching of the Multiply Handicapped Child.* Presented to The Northeast Regional Meeting of The Council for Exceptional Children, Washington, D.C., December, 1964.
8. Minskoff, E. and Minskoff, J.G.: A unified program of remedial and compensatory teaching for children with process learning disabilities. *J Learning Disabil, 9:*215-222, 1976.
9. Roger, R. and Koppmann, M.: The child-oriented resource room. *Except Child, 37:*460-462, 1971.
10. Wiederholt, J.L.: Planning resource rooms for the mildly handicapped. *Focus Except Child, 5,8:* 1974.

CHAPTER 6.

MULTIFAMILY THERAPY

Abraham Lurie, Ph.D.

FAMILY THERAPY

Viewing the family as a group with significant influence on development of children is by no means a new endeavor. The use and analysis of family life with reference to processes, particularly group processes, responsible for mental health or illness of individual members has been an area of study and concern as long as dynamic psychology has been in existence.

There have been several specialities developed with reference to the use of group process in this connection, chief of which is family therapy, and more recently, multifamily therapy. There is a great variation in the structure, styles of work, goals, and techniques of therapists who use family process. Most therapists seem to find and have an agreement about several characteristics of family and multifamily group process that emphasize helping individuals, as well as the family itself, to become involved in a therapeutic process.

Perhaps the most significant characteristic of multifamily group process is the development of strong group cohesiveness. As the multifamily group process develops, the cohesiveness of the members into one group becomes increasingly evident. The group cohesiveness serves as a superego and helps to generate ego strengths for individual members. But more importantly, it gives to individuals and families within the multifamily group itself, after the cohesiveness has been established, a point of reference against which to measure their own strengths. As the process continues, the cohesiveness continues to be a significant factor.

Another characteristic of the multifamily group process is that there must be active therapeutic intervention on the part of the leaders. Unlike many of the more traditional psychotherapeutic approach in the one-to-one relationship, the therapist in the multifamily therapy process needs to be constantly involved and active. The therapist must be aware of many of the relationships that are developed and the significance of these relationships in terms of alliances and subgroups that emerge as the process continues.

It is for this reason that another characteristic in multifamily group process emerges. Experience has led to the belief that cotherapists are more beneficial than a single therapist. Cotherapists are better able to handle the intensity and extent of transfer and countertransfers in multiple family situations. The situations which are likely to emerge within a multifamily situation can more easily influence and perhaps unconsciously affect the solo therapist's relationship to members of the group. A cotherapist is more important to check and to balance involvement when the therapist becomes too directly involved with several members.

Another characteristic is that, as the families get involved in the multiple-family therapy session, the improvement is often related to changes that occur through action rather than through gaining insight. Thus, the families emerge as subgroups within the multifamily group itself and, as such, begin to act on what they perceive to be the problems that they have to face. These actions occur as a result of, not through gaining insight into the dynamics of each of the participants, but rather through the action involved in immediate problem solving and the quality of the relationships formed with other members. Another characteristic of the multifamily group process is that communication between children and adults becomes more open and direct. The multifamily therapy process enables this communication, because children and adults can perceive relationships that occur within other families and begin to act with these perceptions as a frame of reference.

Most therapists agree that the multifamily group process engenders an implicit network of help. The families involved in the therapy process become therapeutic extenders of themselves.

As the group cohesiveness develops, the members of the group begin to seek each other out and to test against one another their own perceptions of what they perceive as problems and use each other as problem solvers. But perhaps even more important is the development of a network of people who, because of their common interest and need to resolve similar problems, begin to feel, consciously and unconsciously, that they are now a part of a network of those who are seeking and at the same time giving help.

The multiple-family group applies opportunity for universal human experience, particularly in terms of relating to one another. Distortion of relationships, as well as difficulties in communication, are some of the more common problems that exist in families and help create patterns of reaction causing difficulties for persons within such families to cope with problems. The multiple-family process offers a field in which individuals and families as groups can test their experience in an accepting and understanding atmosphere. As family members begin to learn how to relate to one another without becoming either self-destructive or destructive of or hurtful to others, this learning becomes transferable to situations outside of the multiple-family group.

Some criteria which can be used to determine whether multiple family as opposed to either individual or family therapy should be utilized are as follows:

CRITERIA FOR USE OF MULTIPLE FAMILY THERAPY

1. Since multiple family-therapy does involve many more persons than the other more conventional forms, there are some therapists who prefer to begin therapy using other modalities such as group, marital-group or individual-family therapy. For some reason, these methods may not appear to be complete or perhaps have not been successful. Multiple-family therapy may offer the individual family an opportunity to get involved in a larger network, which may be more helpful.

2. Multiple-family therapy can often be used when a rigid family system is invested in maintaining and preserving patterns, particularly in terms of marital and parental-child relationships.

Parents in multiple-family groups seem particularly able to release their parental hold on their own children as they begin to relate to other children in the multiple-family therapy group. Children also appear to be more ready to deal with their own conflicts with parents other than their own. Similarly, couples appear better able to recognize marital conflicts in multifamily therapy.

3. Some families cannot tolerate intensive individual family therapy. Such families will find the multifamily therapy process more conducive to their own behavior. They are more apt to get involved when they perceive that other families are taking the risk and are prepared to have their patterns of behavior, as well as communication patterns, analyzed.

A number of families, particularly those who are relatives of particular groups of persons, such as hospitalized patients or children who have special kinds of problems, are often isolated or feel isolated and need contact with other people who have similar problems, which is provided in multiple-family group sessions.

4. Some families find it extremely helpful to have a network of help that they can use outside of either individual or family therapy sessions, and the socialization inherent in these sessions offers such possibilities.

5. Families often need models or mirrors in order to grow as well as gain support to do reality testing. A considerable advantage of multiple-family therapy is that it can be seen as a combination of group therapy, combined with family therapy, which retains the advantages of both modalities. There are some common characteristics of the multiple-family group with the family group experience and group therapy. Perhaps the most obvious is that the multiple-family therapy is a group experience and provides an arena for the sharing of mutual exploration of common problems. The opportunity to get involved in this kind of experience leads to an emotional investment in the process that leads one usually to be more receptive and more open to self-examination and self-awareness.

The multiple-family group experience, like group therapy, offers opportunities to view problems in a more objective light by hearing them verbalized and by participating in problem solving with those who have similar problems. Group therapy and multiple-family group experience offers the opportunity for the participants in the experience to be in the role of "helper." The role of helper offers the participant an opportunity for ego building and for amassing and mobilizing strengths in order to be helpful. This process often continues so that through helping others one gains strength to cope with difficulties present in every individual's experience.

Finally, the multiple-family group experience has in common with group therapy the opportunity to have peers support the challenge and also the involvement of oneself in the process. Risks, challenges, and difficult and traumatic encounters can more readily receive the support of peers within the group itself.

Although there is a commonality among the processes, there are significant differences. In multiple-family therapy, family and group dynamics are meshed, and new dynamics emerge. Simultaneously, individual components and ego strengths become more powerful. Some of these strengths which can surface as a result are as follows:

1. Families have strong emotional ties; some are healthy, and others are pathological. These appear to be more sensitive in multiple-family sessions. Perhaps it is the observation of similar kinds of involvement on the part of other family members that makes it possible for families to have this growing sensitivity emerge during the multifamily process.

2. There are a variety of set roles, norms, and styles of living which emerge in the multiple-family groups. This is particularly true today when families, as a result of many societal pressures and changing normative behavior patterns, are beginning to cope with problems in a variety of ways. As these emerge in the multiple-family group sessions, the families can test their own way of coping with these problems against those which are perhaps more successful.

3. In multiple-family group sessions, there is an availability of surrogate parental figures, which is particularly important when dealing with parent-child relationships. Children, adolescents,

and even young adults who require role models can find in other adults the surrogate parent who can meet the emotional and practical needs that they require.

4. Families are self-protective and show these strengths in multiple-family sessions. The self-protectiveness of the family can be helpful to those families who are particularly vulnerable either in crisis or when having to cope with difficult problems.

5. Interaction is increased between and among families when a group of families are working together in problem solving. As the interaction is increased, feelings of alienation, loneliness, distrust, and vulnerability tend to become more easily dissipated than when working with solo families.

6. Strong alliances can be formed among the family subgroups, particularly among either adolescent or adult peers. Natural conflicts and greater competition also serve to generate families to grope and to work toward cohesiveness and strength. These alliances help families move in this direction.

7. Socialization is a process enhanced particularly on the peer and family level, and is particularly useful in having communication channels opened. Understanding and a feeling of togetherness emerge. Members of the multifamily therapy groups tend to begin to socialize with each other when given some opportunities to do so. Multiple-family therapists offer a contrast to those group therapists who make it a point not to have members of groups socialize with each other. In contrast, families, while not perhaps overtly encouraged, find ways of participating together in social activities.

8. The multiple-family therapy process enables each individual in the session to have a chance in the presence of his family to try himself out in ways which he would not be able to do on an individual basis. Multiple family therapy sessions enable the families to become more tolerant of behavior which in the past they were not able to do. In addition, the individual is able also to try himself out in ways which may be threatening to families but can be accepted if there is support from other families which are present. There is also an opportunity for action, as well as observation within the family sessions, which accelerates the pro-

cess of integration. The process of integration is important because, in single family or one-to-one therapy, there is no way that one can observe the integration of the insight or verbal problem solving. In multiple-family therapy sessions often there is not only the verbal commitment to ideas generated in these sessions, as a result of problem-solving attempts by multiple-family group members, but because there are interested participants from other families, the need to demonstrate the capacity to do problem solving is enhanced. Actual, concrete examples are often brought in verified by other family members as to ways to cope with very troublesome problems.

9. The extended network of help in– and outside the group session centers around the supportive members in times of crisis. Multiple-family group can be and is used as an extended family system. This is particularly important today when so many nuclear families find themselves without the necessary supporting systems in the community. In the past, the extended family did offer this type of support. For a short period, institutions and agencies set up by various governmental and institutional levels provided substitutes for the extended family support when the kinship system became diluted as a result of many factors. Now that institutional life is undergoing severe change, it is no longer possible for many families to count on these institutions to help with problems. New ways need to be found, and some families are able to cope with these losses by developing internal family strengths. But many families continue to require external strengths, such as that offered by a multiple-family group experience.

Multiple-family group therapy serves as a laboratory for reality testing. Families are viewed as they are, rather than as they want to be seen. In this sense, multiple-family group experience acts as a mirror reflecting the family behavior patterns. These behavioral patterns are more easily observed by others and when reflected back to the families, hopefully, it is possible with good leadership intervention, to provide alternative corrective actions.

11. The reduction of the unequal relationship between par-

ent and children can be achieved in the multiple-family therapy process. During this kind of therapy, the child or young adult is able to assert himself, because of the opportunity to have peer alliances. It is not uncommon, in multiple-family therapy sessions, to see youngsters ally themselves both in the matter of defense but also in the matter of attack against some of the ideology and accepted normative behavioral patterns that have been experienced and are verbalized by their adults. At the same time, parents and the older adults are able to ally themselves with their peers. In this process, they note that they need not be devastatingly beaten by youngsters, but, on the contrary, can get involved with them in a give-and-take experience that can result in developing strengths. These strengths are channeled into dealing and coping with reality problems that all members of therapy groups need to face.

12. The parents in these sessions too can often act out their own childlike feelings with the therapist. Parents who have such feelings are often prevented from doing so in single-family therapy sessions. But when a number of families are present, and one set of parents or even a single parent can risk himself in verbalizing or even acting out infantile feelings of this kind, then other parents can begin to do likewise. Obviously this must be noted carefully by the MFT therapist. When such feelings interfere with the healthy and corrective development of behavior patterns conducive to adding strength, then they need to be pointed out to those involved. But again in the process, the acting out of childlike feelings on the part of adults also helps these adults develop empathic relationships with the younger members of the multiple family therapy groups.

13. There are opportunities in multiple-family group therapy for improving the individual's self-image. Family roles are played out in rigid systems, but the group allows and stimulates the emergence of other feelings that may not have emerged before and are often unknown to oneself and one's family. This can be seen particularly in the development of new roles for different members of the family. This is encouraged, as family members note how members of other families who are participating in the

sessions act out their roles. In addition to the important element of exposure to various roles that the family members develop and use for themselves, the participants can note that they are not heading for destruction or undue criticism which can be ego shattering. On the contrary such participation stimulates participants to try such new roles, to be a more loving parent or to be a more understanding adult.

14. Multiple-family group therapy offers the incorporation into the therapeutic milieu the possibility for use of activities. Since multiple-family therapy sessions involve more persons than individual-family therapy, it is relatively simple to introduce activities and or task oriented sessions. This has many advantages, including the further development of group cohesiveness, because the planning of, participating in, and concluding an activity can bring gratification to all involved. This gratification adds to ego strengths by helping the members conclude an activity in which all have participated and from which all can derive some satisfaction.

15. Marginal families with little motivation will be carried along. The families participating often range from nonsophisticated to very heavily psychologically and introspective family systems. The advantage of including a number of families is for the marginal families whose exposure to family therapy methods have not been either useful or experienced, to observe the helping process and begin to participate with problems at their own pace and at their own level of willingness to participate. The pressure to become involved is not pointed to any single family since there are a number so involved. Some of these families that have originally held back will often become more heavily involved as group cohesiveness develops. With nonparticipating families, the use of activities can be a spur. Some of these families, for example, can and have useful activities skills, and even though the members may not be articulate, the ability to express themselves through activities can be as equally useful in participating and aiding others as the verbal participation.

16. Multiple-family group experience has the potential of taking on the characteristics of the family in which the therapists

can act as parental surrogates when appropriate. Here, there needs to be some very careful consideration given to not manipulating this parental role to the extent of excluding the legitimate parents, particularly when children are involved. This is another reason for having cotherapists involved in multiple-family therapy sessions. But this extended family type, which begins to emerge after a number of sessions, has very definite beneficial effects in terms of enabling the participants to view themselves in this network of relationship much like the old kinship system. The therapists, in their parental role, in some cases, can exert their influence as ego ideals for those who had difficulty in the past identifying with such role models.

Some of the techniques that therapists need to sharpen include the ability to focus on the family, to work with the group as a whole rather than in the one-to-one relationship with which many therapists are trained and have familiarity. Although one works with the group, there can be individual therapeutic interventions from time to time. Perhaps the single most important attribute of a therapist is to have a sense of confidence that can emerge from his own awareness of his role in the family and possibly having experienced family therapy.

As the group begins to coalesce and the workers and or coworkers begin to become involved in the process, then the more active participation of the therapists can be reflected in confrontation in the ability to make connections between families, role and themes, and to be able to point out these connections and observations as they occur.

As the members begin to take on extended therapeutic influence, then the leader can and should become less active in the psychotherapeutic sense. Other techniques can be introduced such as games, gestalt techniques, and transactional and roleplaying methods. Activities including socialization experiences, such as trips, home visiting, even camping or weekend trips can be extremely helpful. As the group gains experience and the members gain confidence in this process, then interventions by the therapists to keep the group focus and to actively help individuals express will become less frequent.

As the process continues, the parents will see each other exhibiting human equalities and not controllers of behavior. The "bad" children, for example, emerge as human beings and some of the "good" children begin to give up their valued turf. Sometimes siblings maintain family patterns and use the group for their own safety and support to confront the parents and make themselves heard and felt as individuals.

CHAPTER 7.

CHILDREN AT RISK FOR PSYCHOPATHOLOGY*

SHELDON WEINTRAUB, Ph.D.
JOHN M. NEALE, Ph.D.

THE STUDY of children at risk for psychopathology is a promising research strategy, designed to identify precursor signs of adult maladjustment and to open the door to possible early inter– and prevention of the debilitating and refractory psychiatric disturbances of adulthood. The high-risk design avoids many of the serious methodological confounds inherent in the study of already maladjusted adults. For example, recollections of the adult patient and his family concerning possible etiological factors are suspect because of the notoriously low reliability and validity of data collected retrospectively. Psychological and biological laboratory research with adult patients and control groups still fails to control adequately for the correlates of psychopathology, such as institutionalization, medication, social failure, and personal suffering.[26] Any difference found between the patient and the control groups may well represent a consequent of the disorder rather than a cause. An example can be drawn from the area of psychophysiology. A number of investigators have reported that schizophrenics have higher heart rates than controls, e.g. hospital attendants. This evidence has most often been taken to mean that schizophrenics are at higher than normal arousal levels. But the relationship itself may be spurious—hospitalized schizophrenics are notoriously sedentary, and lack of exercise leads to higher heart rate. The study of high-risk children prior to the development of manifest psychopathology is not biased by the conse-

*This paper was supported by Grant MH-21145 from The National Institute of Mental Health and by funds from the Grant Foundation.

quents of the disorder or the distortions of retrospective reporting. Longitudinal follow-up of these children into adulthood may lead to the discovery of factors that identify those who break down.

The Stony Brook High-Risk Project[32] focuses specifically on children vulnerable to schizophrenia, the most prevalent and incapacitating of the psychiatric disorders. The definition of high risk is founded on the well-established empirical relationship between schizophrenia in a parent and the likelihood that the child of such a parent will be maladjusted. Approximately 50 percent of children with a schizophrenic parent will be psychiatrically maladjusted in adulthood, with about 10 to 15 percent diagnosed as schizophrenic.[18] The purpose of this paper is to describe the methods used in the Stony Brook High-Risk Project and to present some of our preliminary findings.

OVERVIEW

The purpose of the first stage in this two-stage project is to provide a complete description of the adjustment—in terms of strengths and weaknesses—of children vulnerable to psychopathology. New admissions to several local psychiatric facilities are screened to determine if they have children in school. If so, an appointment is arranged, the project is explained to the patient, and consent is obtained. The patient is then assessed in detail. Shortly thereafter, the patient's spouse is contacted and an appointment made to visit the home. At that time, the spouse is evaluated in detail. Finally, another home visit is arranged, after the patient has returned home. During this visit information on the marriage and family functioning is collected, as well as some information on the children involved. During these home visits, permission is obtained to evaluate the children at school, and appointments are set up for the children to come to our laboratories at the University.* Our sample now consists of ninety-one families with a schizophrenic parent (sixty mothers and thirty-one fathers) and 200 children, fifty-eight families with a depressed

---

*The same assessment procedures are also administered to control families. The method of selecting controls is described later in the section on school assessment.

parent (thirty-six mothers and twenty-two fathers) and 120 children, and sixty control families with 125 children. Although the target figure for the authors' cross-sectional sample is almost met, they are continuing to sample new families, particularly those with a hospitalized father.

The second stage of the project involves a longitudinal investigation of the vulnerable children. Families are contacted every six months to maintain contact and continuity. Follow-up studies in both the school and our laboratory are conducted every two years, employing the same assessment procedures that are currently in use. Only by studying these children longitudinally may childhood characteristics predictive of adult psychopathology be discovered. This information will greatly increase understanding of the development of schizophrenia and also open the door to early intervention programs.

A more detailed description of the different aspects of the project, indicating for each the rationale for the various procedures will be given.

ASSESSMENT OF PATIENTS

Two patient-parent variables are investigated: (1) diagnosis (schizophrenia, depressive, and normal) and (2) sex (mother, father). The primary focus of the study is on the children of a schizophrenic parent, but by including another psychiatric group, the effects of being reared by a psychiatric patient may be controlled, while the effects of a possible schizophrenic genotype and specific schizophrenic rearing behaviors are allowed to vary. The children of male, as well as female, psychiatric patients are studied to provide a more complete sample and allow the relationship between sex of patient and sex of child on the child's adjustment to be examined.

The official diagnosis provides only a starting point in the assessment of patients. A full and detailed assessment of each patient is conducted for the following reasons: (1) to increase the reliability and validity of the psychiatric diagnosis; (2) to obtain constant descriptive data by asking the same questions to all patients; (3) to obtain actual behavioral descriptions of subjects, rather than only diagnostic labels, which will allow analyses such as a comparison of the specific nature of the behavior problems of the parent, e.g., withdrawal or acting out, with those of his children; (4) to provide measures of premorbid status and social competence; (5) to provide an evaluation from several sources: (a) self, (b) spouse, and (c) diagnostician.

Diagnoses are made using the following information: (1) Current and Past Psychopathology Scales (CAPPS),[44] a structured interview schedule that yields a computer diagnosis; (2) Mini-Mult,[21] a brief version of the MMPI; (3) Patient Adjustment Scale-Spouse Informant[32] an assessment of the patient from the perspective of the spouse; and (4) an abstract of hospital records. For a case to be included, two trained diagnosticians working independently had to agree on the diagnosis and assign a confidence rating of 1 or 2 on a 4-point scale.

ASSESSMENT OF THE SPOUSE AND HOME ENVIRONMENT

A complete assessment of the entire family unit is essential; the psychiatric patient-parent is not the sole influence on his child. When one parent develops a psychosis, the quality of the adjustment of the spouse may exert a critical influence on the adjustment of the children. It thus seems imperative to obtain a detailed assessment of the spouse, and, to this end, the same instruments and procedures as are used with the psychiatric parent are administered to the spouse: (1) CAPPS, (2) Mini-Mult, and (3) Spouse Adjustment Scale-Patient Informant. As with the assessment of the patient, evaluation of the spouse includes not only information obtained by self-report, but also information as perceived and reported by the patient on psychopathology and role functioning. This information is tape recorded and collected during the home visits.

The total environment is another factor expected to exert an influence on the adaptation of the children. For example, in the Judge-Baker studies of the adult status of children seen at a clinic, no healthy marriages (characterized by "mutuality") were noted in the families in which the child later became schizophrenic. Marriages characterized by mutual withdrawal, minimal interaction, separate bedrooms, and overt hostility and distrust were much more frequent.[53] Social isolation was also common in the families of the preschizophrenic. In our study, marital adjustment is evaluated by the Short Marital Adjustment Test.[24] Family functioning is assessed by the Family Evaluation Schedule, a modification of the St. Paul Scale of Family Functioning[14] and the Family Evaluation Scale.[45] The schedule measures family functioning in seven categories: (1) family relations and family unity, (2) effects of patient's problems on the family, (3) care and training of children, (4) social activities, (5) economic practices, (6) household practices, and (7) health conditions and practices.

Administration of the Scale requires approximately two hours of interviewing and is the major purpose of one of the home visits. The Marital Adjustment Test and Family Evaluation Schedules provide broad descriptive information concerning the home environment, as well as permitting an evaluation of particular family patterns identified in previous research with preschizophrenics.

A summary of our assessment procedures to be applied to the patient families and control families is presented in Table 7-I.

As already mentioned, a primary purpose of the home visits

TABLE 7-I

ASSESSMENT PROCEDURES FOR PARENTS OF TARGET AND CONTROL GROUPS

	Psychiatric Diagnostic Procedures	*Measures of Family Functioning*

Patient	CAPPS
	MMPI
	Patient Adjustment
	   Scale-Spouse Informant
		Short Marital
		   Adjustment Test
		Family Evaluation
		   Schedule

Patient's
Spouse
	CAPPS
	MMPI
	Spouse Adjustment
	   Scale-Patient Informant
		Short Marital
		   Adjustment Test
		Family Evaluation
		   Schedule

Control
Parents
	CAPPS
	MMPI
	Spouse Adjustment
	   Scale-Patient Informant
		Short Marital
		   Adjustment Test
		Family Evaluation
		   Schedule

is to assess the "normal" spouse in detail. A preliminary examination of the male spouses of schizophrenic, depressed, and controls in the sample[7] used the CAPPS, Mini-Mult, and Marital Adjustment Test. On the CAPPS, the husbands of schizophrenic and depressed women reported more role impairment (wage earner, mate, and father) than did the controls. Analysis of the Mini-Mult revealed only one significant effect; husbands of schizophrenics were higher than other groups on the K-scale, suggesting greater defensiveness on their part. Analysis of the Marital Adjustment Test revealed large differences in marital satisfaction; husbands of schizophrenics were most dissatisfied, followed by husbands of depressives, and then controls. These results do not reflect diagnosable psychopathology in the spouses of psychiatric patients. These husbands are impaired, however, in carrying out their usual role functions and express much dissatisfaction with their marriages. Perhaps both these findings are only transient disturbances reflecting the impact of hospitalization of the wife. Our follow-up assessments will allow this issue to be clarified.

ASSESSMENT OF CHILDREN

In turning to our assessment of the children, we must first note that the offspring of schizophrenics are *not* grossly deviant as young children. The data available suggests that while high-risk children can be discriminated from others, the differences are going to be subtle.[13] How then may variables be selected that will allow the children at risk to be discriminated from controls and be predictive of later psychopathology? The first strategy is based on the continuity approach, in which it is assumed that there will be similarities between the behavior of adult schizophrenics and preschizophrenic children. A search for early indicators of symptomatic behavior through downward extensions of laboratory variables shown to be important in studies of adult schizophrenics is done. On a descriptive level, for example, one might expect to find that preschizophrenic children are socially withdrawn and that this withdrawal is a precursor of the aversion of interpersonal relationships displayed by adult schizophrenics.

Retrospective and follow-back studies have, in fact, found that many schizophrenics are described as having been extremely shy, introverted, withdrawn, or "shut-in" personalities as childern.[10,11, 19,36,56] But, follow-up studies find that children referred for withdrawal are no more likely to become schizophrenic than are normal subjects.[29,30]

Similarly, Mednick and Schulsinger[27] found that although children of schizophrenic mothers were more withdrawn than controls, among the high-risk children there was no relationship between childhood withdrawal and later psychopathology. A minimal criterion for judging the importance of a child behavior in high-risk research is that children who exhibit it are more likely than average to become schizophrenic. Withdrawal, then, does not meet this criterion.

How can one account for the fact that withdrawal seems to show important continuity in follow-back studies but none in follow-up studies? Two possibilities present themselves. First, withdrawal may not be a stable characteristic, even though introversion and passivity are relatively stable temperamental characteristics.[27,25] Indeed, the assumption that any childhood sign of emotional disturbance (as opposed to cognitive or behavioral problems, e.g. antisocial behavior) is predictive of later maladjustment may be challenged. Kohlberg, LaCrosse, and Ricks[22] view emotional-symptomatic behavior as (1) having no regular age-developmental trends, (2) having little adaptational value and few direct environmental consequences, and (3) as being highly dependent upon current developmental and situational influences of the family, school, and peer groups. Thus, symptomatic traits such as withdrawal are relatively transitory, with whatever stability they exhibit a function of the temperamental aspects of the trait. A transitory state is unlikely to be useful predictively.

Second, there may be a semantic conceptual difference between the behaviors labeled "withdrawn" in childhood, and those behaviors implicated in schizophrenia that are labeled "withdrawn."[38] Withdrawal characterized by shyness, introversion, passivity, and discomfort in social situations may not be the same as active seclusion or avoidance of social contact.

Another argument against a continuity approach does not

question the assumption of continuity per se, but focuses on the narrowness of this approach. Trying to find developmental precursors of schizophrenia in the children of schizophrenic parents is a worthwhile but limited goal. It is known, for example, that in addition to being at risk for schizophrenia, these children are also at risk for retarded intellectual development, sociopathy, and neurosis.[18] A broader assessment could provide valuable information on the etiology of these disorders as well. But if a continuity approach is not adopted, on what basis should variables be selected?

One successful attempt at long-range prediction has been labeled *developmental-adaptational.*[22] This approach, which constitutes a second strategy, views the child's behavior as reflections of appropriate coping mechanisms, rather than as reflections of fixed character traits. It focuses on the development of *general competence behaviors,* usually with cognitive components, that have direct adaptational significance. Developmental-adaptive behaviors are cumulative, age-developmental, and, because of the cognitive components, have direct adaptational significance. Developmental-adaptive behaviors are cumulative, age-developmental, and, because of the cognitive ability components, more or less irreversible. In addition, positive adaptive behaviors are supported and rewarded by the environment (most importantly in school achievement and self-esteem), whereas the absence of symptomatic behavior is not.

Adaptive behaviors have been found to be more effective predictors of later adjustment than symptomatic behaviors. For example, Kellam and Schiff[20] found that ratings by teachers on adaptive tasks (social contact, authority acceptance, maturation, cognitive achievement, concentration, and global adaptation) although correlated with symptomatic ratings by clinicians, were better predictors of later ratings, both adaptive and symptomatic, than were symptomatic ratings. Thus, symptomatic-emotional problems may well be more of a consequence than a cause of developmental-adaptive difficulties.

How then can developmental-adaptive variables be selected that will predict later psychopathology? A partial answer may be found in the large-scale programs involved in the early identification of maladaptive behavior in young school children,[3,8] which have proved quite successful. These programs typically use an amalgam of screening techniques with the most effective predictors being teacher ratings, peer ratings, IQ, academic achievement (particularly in arithmetic), age-grade relationship, and rate of absence.

Assessment of the Children in School

The county in which the authors work does not have a centralized school system, and, therefore, all forty of the local school districts had to be contacted separately, and thirty-eight of these boards agreed to participate. A plan was worked out so that the confidentiality of subjects and their families is maintained. The reason for our choice of children is concealed from those who have daily contact with them. These persons are told only that this study is concerned with the academic and social competence of school children in the county and that subjects are selected on a random basis. Two control groups are selected once target children are located in their classrooms. One of these is a same-sex but otherwise randomly drawn child from the same classroom; the other is matched to the target child on sex, age, race, social class, and IQ. Families of control children were contacted later to secure participation in other phases of the study (the family assessment and laboratory studies), until a total of sixty control families were obtained. The two control groups are necessary since, on the one hand, matching is desirable as a control for possible confounding, e.g. the groups could differ on social class, while, on the other hand, matched variables may not be merely peripheral correlates of schizophrenia. Matching on social class, for example, involves the tacit assumption that social class is "not really" relevant to schizophrenia. This assumption may not be warranted; hence, a random control group is desirable.[28]

Intelligence and Academic Performance

School achievement has been demonstrated to be predictive of general maladjustment[17,49] and may also provide a partial downward extension of the social competence variable,[35] which has proven so useful in investigations of adult schizophrenics. Information already available in the child's school record is utilized to assess academic and intellectual functioning. Achievement test scores, academic performance records, attendance records, teacher comments, and IQ scores are collected.

Social Adjustment and Interpersonal Competence

Since the social concomitants of schizophrenia are so clear, it is plausible to expect some early indications of social deficits in the behavior of high-risk children. Peer relations are an especially appropriate avenue for the measurement of interpersonal competence. Interactions with peers constitute the most significant social arena a child encounters, outside of his family. Furthermore, school situations (classroom and playground) are representative of the work, competitive, and social demands with which the child will later have to cope. They are measured in a nontest context of the child's real life environment and are made by multiple observers with whom the child has differing personal relationships, and who consequently view him from varying perspectives.[43] Peer ratings are stable over time[41] and have been validated by teacher ratings, behavioral observation, and clinician ratings.[1,50,55] Low endorsement by peers is associated with poor adjustment and poor utilization of academic abilities.[16] Peer relations are also effective predictors of later maladjustment,[17,39] and more specifically of schizophrenia.[27]

The authors have developed their peer nomination procedure. The choice of behaviors to be evaluated was determined by their (1) role in childhood and adult maladjustment, especially schizophrenia, (2) identification by previous factor analytic studies, and (3) similarity to behaviors factorially defined by the Devereux Behavior Rating Scales, completed by the child's teachers and parents. Thus, evaluations from peers, teachers, and parents may be compared as directly as possible. The format consists of an item by peer matrix, in which the items appear as rows down the left side of the page and the names of the children in the class across the top of the page. The subject checks each child he believes to be described by a particular item. Only those students of the same sex as the target child are rated by both the boys and girls in the class. After rating the other children in the class, each child also completes a self-evaluation. Factor analysis of the scale has revealed three major dimensions: (1) aggressive disruptiveness, (2) withdrawal, and (3) popularity and likeability.[34]

Social adjustment is also being assessed by teacher ratings of the target children and their matched and random controls. The instrument selected for use is the Devereux Elementary School Behavior Rating Scale.[47] It consists of a series of items in which the teacher compares the child being rated to other children using either a five- or seven-point rating scale. The scale was specifically designed to allow the teacher to rate the overt behavior (rather than internal processes) of the child in a normal classroom. It consists of forty-seven items that define eleven factors: classroom disturbance, impatience, disrespect-defiance, external blame, achievement anxiety, external reliance, comprehension, inattentive-withdrawn, irrelevant-responsiveness, creative initiative, and needs closeness to teacher.

To ensure the anonymity of the target child, the teacher completes a very brief child behavior rating form on every child in the class of the same sex as the target child. The teacher is told that a comparison of the utility of this brief behavior rating procedure with the considerably longer Devereux Scale which she is asked to complete on just three children who were selected "randomly" (target child, matched control, random control) is being made. Preliminary analyses of a sample of 58 offspring of schizophrenic mothers, 43 of depressive mothers, and 114 controls showed that the former two groups could be discriminated from the latter on seven of the eleven Devereux factors.[55] The two groups with patient mothers exhibited higher levels of classroom disturbance, impatience, disrespect-defiance, and inattentiveness-withdrawal. Their teachers also rated them as showing low comprehension, creative initiative, and relatedness to teacher. This pattern is quite similar to a profile type found by Spivack, Swift, and Prewitt[48] in their analysis of classroom behavior. They describe children with such a profile as presenting a major behavioral disturbance. These children manifest acting out and impulsive behavior and are in conflict with the behavioral demands of the classroom. Such children seemed unable to make productive use of the classroom and performed poorly.

Notably, teachers did not discriminate children of schizophrenic from children of depressive mothers. Even though the behavior pattern of the offspring of schizophrenic mothers was similar to that reported in other studies, our data suggest that these characteristics may not be specific to children of schizophrenic mothers.

Assessment of Children by Parents

The child's social adjustment as perceived by his father and mother is also evaluated. The parents complete the Devereux Child Behavior Rating Scale[46] to describe the manifest behavior pathology of their children. The Scale is directly comparable to the Devereux School Behavior Rating Scale and consists of a series of items on which the parent rates his child on either a five- or seven-point rating scale. It consists of ninety-seven items that define seventeen factors: distractability, poor self-care, pathological use of senses, emotional detachment, social isolation, poor coordination and body tonus, incontinence, messiness and sloppiness, inadequate need for independence, unresponsiveness to stimulation, proneness to emotional upset, need for adult contact, anxious-fearful ideation, "impulse" ideation, inability to delay, social aggression, and unethical behavior.

Laboratory Studies

Many hypotheses concerning processes relevant to the etiology of schizophrenia cannot be evaluated on the basis of descriptive data. Processes such as attention dysfunction,[42,52] cognitive slippage, and extreme sensitivity to censure[12] can be assessed only through studies specifically designed to tap them. Thus, several experimental studies designed to test hypotheses concerning more specific variables that may be crucially important in normal childhood development and in the etiology of schizophrenia are being conducted.

Two children per day are tested, Mondays through Thursdays.

Children whose parents balk at their missing school are tested on Saturdays. The children are picked up at home by a project staff member at about 8:30 AM, taken out to lunch at midday, and returned home at about 3:30 PM. A letter describing the results of our assessment is sent to the parents, and if any problem seems severe enough, an appropriate referral is made. Although parents are apprised of the *experimental* nature of the measures that are used, they seem quite interested in and grateful for this attention.

Wechsler Intelligence Scale For Children (WISC)

As school records began to be collected, the authors found that many children in their sample did not have an adequate intelligence estimate already in their file. Thus, the WISC was included in our assessment battery. Due to time limitations, however, the full WISC could not be administered. Based on several validity studies of short forms of the WISC, the authors decided to use the most reliable tetrad: block design, picture arrangement, and information and vocabulary.

Information Processing

In recent years, attention dysfunction has been viewed as a prominent aspect of the process (es) underlying the cognitive malfunctioning of adult schizophrenics.[31] Recent data point toward an explanation of this inefficient processing in terms of an inability among schizophrenic patients to apply different processing operations to relevant versus irrelevant information. This ability to ignore irrelevant input has been viewed by Eleanor Gibson as a key process in perceptual development: "As the child matures, he is better able to select out and use those properties that serve to distinguish things from one another and are adapted to his task, and to disregard nonessential properties."[15]

A parallel seems evident between the attention dysfunction found in schizophrenic adults and a process that is critically relevant to perceptual development. This study follows up this parallel by examining visual search in the samples of children of schizophrenic parents, children of depressive parents, and control children.

The task involves searching down a list of thirty letter-strings of four letters each. The lists are mounted on cardboard backing so that they can be inserted into a light-tight box behind a half-silvered mirror. On a ready signal from *E,* the child presses a button which illuminates lamps, making the display visible and activating a clock-counter. She then searches down the list and upon finding the target presses the button again. This second button press turns off the lamps and stops the clock-counter. The elapsed time from the first to the second button press provides the index of search time.

Twenty displays were constructed, each containing the letter *G* along with low-confusability, irrelevant letters — *K, M, A, L, N,* and *X.* Twenty parallel displays were constructed employing high-confusability, irrelevant letters — *J, B, S, R, Q* and *C.* Within each type of display, the target letter appears five times in each of the quadrants. Each child is presented with each display once, with a different random order of display presentations for each child.

Distractibility

Another task related to attentional processes has been adapted from the work of Chapman and McGhie.[4] They found that adding a distracting voice to a digit span test created a test that had great power in discriminating schizophrenic patients from other groups of subjects. In our no-distraction condition, children are presented with standard instructions for the digit span test; digits are then presented at a one per two-second rate, and the child tries to report as much as he can after listening to the series. In the distraction condition, the one-second interval between each relevant digit is filled by an opposite-sexed voice saying an irrelevant digit. The use of a standardized test, such as the digit span, allows the test to be tailored to the age-range of the subjects being used in the present study. Specifically, children in grades one and two receive four-digit chains, children in grades three and four receive five-digit chains, and subjects above the fifth grade receive six-digit chains. Each child receives ten distraction trials and ten no-distraction trials.

Object Sorting

Another measure which has been extensively used as an index of schizophrenic thought disorder is object sorting. Tutko and Spence,[51] for example, devised a scoring system for the Goldstein-Scheerer test that discriminates between normal, brain injured, and good and poor premorbid schizophrenics. An object sorting test is particularly applicable to a high-risk study, because it is easily administered to children of different ages and extensive developmental data have already been collected.[33]

The specific task the authors use was devised by Olver and Hornsby.[33] A child is shown an array of forty-two drawings of objects, such as an apple, a fish, a clock, and a boat, etc. He is then asked to select a group of pictures that are alike in some way and then give the reason for his choice. Ten trials are administered. Each sorting is categorized into one of four types — *superordinate, complexive, vague,* and *thematic.* Superordinate groupings are based on a common feature shared by each member of a group. Complexive groupings are based in local rather than universal characteristics within the group, e.g. "banana and peach are yellow, peach and potato are round, potato and meat are served together." A thematic grouping occurs when items are linked together in a story, e.g. "I put on my *shoes,* used my *comb,* and left the *house.*" A vague response represents an attempt to specify a common attribute but is overgeneralized or only loosely related to the object.

Word Communication

Deviant language, and by inference, thought processes, have been among the most researched topics in adult schizophrenics. Recently, Cohen and Cahmi[6] have used a word-communication task to assess referential thinking in adult schizophrenics. One subject, the speaker, provides a single, one-word clue that will allow a listener to determine which of two words is the referent. The listener tries to guess, on the basis of the clue, which of the two words is the referent. For example, the speaker might be shown the pair *car—automobile* with car designated as the referent. The speaker's task is to provide a one-word clue to allow the listener to guess that car and not automobile is correct. For this pair, clues such as *drive* and *wheels* would be ineffective while *hop* and *box* would provide discriminating, helpful information to the listener. In their investigation, Cohen and Cahmi found that schizophrenics performed more poorly than controls only in the speaker role.

In adapting this task for children, the main requirement was forming pairs of words so that the children would understand the words and have knowledge sufficient to provide adequate clues. This was accomplished by drawing on the large literature on word knowledge in children and by pilot testing. Drawing on Chapman's theory of verbal behavior in schizophrenia[5] two types of pairs were constructed. One type had a low-meaning associate as the "best" cue, e.g. *bat*-stick — to which the low-meaning but very effective clue is *animal*. In the other type of item, the effective cue is **not** a low-meaning response, e.g. king-*president,* to which an effective but non-low-meaning response could be America. Each of the twenty word pairs is presented to the subjects who are instructed to think of a clue to allow another child to know which of the two words is the referent. Clues are scored on a three-point scale: 0 = inadequate, 1 = adequate, 2 = good.

Emotional Responding

A study of schizophrenia would be incomplete without some assessment of emotionality. Several high-risk studies have attempted this by assessing psychophysiological responses to stressful stimuli, such as loud noises. The authors have opted for an approach which is different in two respects. First, the stimulus materials presented to the children are those hypothesized to be relevant to the development of schizophrenia, e.g. family scenes involving conflict and communication inadequacies. Second, rather than testing psychophysiological responses, the authors have chosen to monitor the child's facial response to these situations.

Two ten-minute films were constructed. The first depicts a positive family interaction. A child returns home from school late and then tearfully explains that his/her bicycle is missing.

The parents respond in an understanding way, and the scene ends with the beginnings of action to try to find the lost bicycle. The second film shows a family interaction characterized primarily by unclear communication and conflict. Each film was shot twice, with either a male or female child, so that the sex of the child in the film was always the same as that of the child viewing.

The films are presented by videotape onto a television monitor. While the child is watching the film, a camera located behind a one-way screen photographs the child's face. A filmed record of the child's facial reactions is then fed to a special-effects generator, which produces another video tape having a split-screen effect with the child's face on one side and the material he is viewing on the other. Subsequently, the child's facial responses are scored using the reliable coding procedure developed by Ekman, Friesen, and Ellsworth.[9]

Interpersonal Competence

Although interpersonal competence, as measured by peer relations, is being assessed in the schools, a more fine-grained laboratory analysis of the core components of peer relations would seem to be warranted. The authors have decided to measure altruism, cooperation, and competition in a two-person game situation. Our tasks measure the child's willingness to share and his problem-solving strategies in a prisoner's dilemma game where a stooge is programmed to behave either cooperatively or competitively. The prisoner's dilemma game is the most common two-person, non-zero-sum game used in experimental studies of problem solving, social interaction, and conflict processes.[37] The dilemma posed for the players is that what is best for each individual is not best for both of them. This characteristic of the game has at least a logical similarity to many "real-world" conflicts.[37]

The first stage of the game is a measure of altruism. For twenty trials, the stooge responds first, and the subject learns of that choice. He thus is in control of how much he will win and how much his partner will win; he can either share or keep all of the winnings for himself. The task then changes to a measure of problem-solving strategy, cooperativeness, and competitiveness. The "partners" respond simultaneously, and thus the subject must choose before learning about his partner's choice. The stooge is programmed for twenty trials with a tit-for-tat strategy, consistently reciprocating the subject's behavior. If the subject does not adopt a cooperative strategy and attempts to exploit his partner, his overall payoff is compromised. In the third stage, the stooge suddenly switches to an unconditionally competitive strategy for twenty trials. If the subject does not also adopt a competitive strategy to counteract his partner, he receives no payoff. From the pattern of the subject's responses, his/her coping and problem-solving skills in an "interpersonal" situation can be assessed.

Report of Parental Behavior

In the lab, the revised Child's Report of Parental Behavior Inventory (CRPBI),[40] an instrument specifically designed to assess parental behavior from the viewpoint of the child, is individually administered. Numerous factor analyses with a variety of populations have consistently yielded three orthogonal factors. The first factor labeled *acceptance-rejection* is self-explanatory; the other two, *psychological autonomy-psychological control* and *firm control-lax control,* represent two types of parental control — covert, intrusive, psychological control or overt rule making, limit setting, and enforcement, respectively. An analysis of the CRPBI ratings of three groups of children, those with a schizophrenic parent (n = 150), those with a depressive parent (n = 117), and those whose parents had no psychiatric history (n = 141), has recently been completed.[54]

Schizophrenic mothers were perceived more positively (accepting and child centered) by their children than were normal mothers and more lax in the discipline of their children than were depressed mothers. Depressed mothers were also more child centered than normal mothers. Schizophrenic fathers tended to be viewed more negatively by their children than normal fathers. Husbands of schizophrenic women were viewed as strict disciplinarians and husbands of depressed women as controlling their children through guilt.

Conclusions

The high-risk method offers great promise as a research strategy for investigating the development of schizophrenia. Data is collected before the onset of problems so the information is not biased by the consequents of schizophrenia, e.g., drug treatment or institutionalization, or the inherent limitations of retrospective reporting. The information thus obtained may also be useful for early detection and intervention programs. In this paper, the authors have described a comprehensive high-risk study with several important features. A depressive control is included and patients, spouses, and the family are assessed in detail. Children are assessed from several vantage points — the home, school, and laboratory.

REFERENCES

1. Bonney, M.E.: Social behavior differences between second grade children of high and low sociometric status. *J Educ Res, 48:*481-495, 1955.
2. Bower, E.M.: *Early Identification of Emotionally Handicapped Children in School,* 2nd ed. Springfield, Thomas, 1969.
3. Brownbridge, P. and Van Vleet, P. (Eds.): *Investments in Prevention: The Prevention of Learning and Behavior Problems in Young Children.* San Francisco, Pace ID Center, 1969.
4. Chapman, J.S. and McGhie, A.: A comparative study of disordered attention in schizophrenia. *J Ment Sci, 108:*487, 500, 1962.
5. Chapman, L.J., Chapman, J.P., and Miller, G.: A theory of verbal behavior in schizophrenia. In Maher, B.A. (Ed.): *Progress in Experimental Personality Research.* New York, Acad Pr, 1964, vol. I.
6. Cohen, B.D. and Camhi, J.: Schizophrenic performance in a word communication task. *J Abnorm Psychol, 72:*240-246, 1967.
7. Cohen, S.: *Comparison Among Schizophrenic, Depressive, and Normal Spouses.* Unpublished dissertation. State University of New York at Stony Brook, 1974.
8. Cowen, E.L., Izzo, A.D., Miles, H., Telschow, E.F., Trost, M.A., and Zax, M.: A mental health program in the school setting: Description and evaluation. *J Psychol, 56:*307-356, 1963.
9. Ekman, P., Friesan, W.V., and Ellsworth, P.: *Emotion in the Human Face.* Elmsford, New York, Pergamon, 1971.
10. Frazee, H.E.: Children who later became schizophrenic. *Smith College Studies in Social Work, 23:*125-149, 1953.
11. Friedlander, D.: Personality development of 27 children who later became psychotic. *J Abnorm Soc Psychol, 40:*330-335, 1945.

12. Garmezy, N.: The prediction of performance in schizophrenia. In Hoch, P.N. and Zubin, J. (Eds.): *Psychopathology of Schizophrenia.* New York, Grune, 1966.

13. Garmezy, N. and Streitman, S.: Children at risk: The search for the antecedents of schizophrenia. *Schizophrenia Bull, 8:*14-90, 1974.

14. Geismar, L.L. and Ayres, B.: *Measuring Family Functionings: A Manual on a Method for Evaluating the Social Functioning of Disordered Families.* St. Paul, Family Centered Project, The Greater St. Paul Community Chest and Councils, Inc., 1960.

15. Gibson, E.: *Principles of Perceptual Development.* New York, Appleton, 1969, p. 462.

16. Hartup, W.W., Glazer, J.A., and Charlesworth, R.: Peer reinforcement and sociometric status. *Child Dev, 38:*1010-1024, 1967.

17. Havighurst, R.J., Bowman, P.H., Liddie, G.P., Matthews, C.V., and Pierce, J.V.: *Growing Up in River City.* New York: Wiley, 1962.

18. Heston, L.L.: Psychiatric disorders in foster home reared children of schizophrenic mothers. *Br J Psychiatry, 112:*819-825, 1966.

19. Kasanin, J. and Veo, L.: A study of the school adjustment of children who later in life became psychotic. *Am J Orthopsychiatry, 2:*212-230, 1932.

20. Kellam, S.G., and Schiff, S.K.: Adaptation and mental illness in the first-grade classrooms of an urban community. *Psychiatr Res Rep, 21:* 79-91, 1967.

21. Kincannon, J.C.: Prediction of the standard MMPI scale scores from 71 items: The Mini-Mult. *J. Consult Clin Psychol, 35:*126-127, 1968.

22. Kohlberg, L., La Crosse, J., and Ricks, D.: The predictability of adult mental health from child behavior. In Wolman, B. (Ed.): *Manual of Child Psychopathology.* New York, McGraw, 1972.

23. Kohn, M.L.: Social class and schizophrenia. In Rosenthal, D. and Kety, S. (Eds.) : *The Transmission of Schizophrenia.* Elmsford, New York, Pergamon, 1968.

24. Locke, H.J. and Wallace, K.M.: Short marital adjustment and prediction tests: Their reliability and validity. *Marriage and Family Living, 21:* 251-255, 1959.

25. Macfarlane, J.W., Allen, C., and Honzik, M.P.: *A Developmental Study of the Behavior Problems of Normal Children Between Twenty-one Months and Fourteen Years.* Berkeley and Los Angeles, University of California Press, 1954.

26. Mednick, S.A. and McNeil, T.F.: Current methodology in research on the etiology of schizophrenia: Serious difficulties which suggest the use of the high-risk-group method. *Psychol Bull, 70:*681-693, 1968.

27. Mednick, S.A. and Schulsinger, F.: Some premorbid characteristics related to breakdown in children with schizophrenic mothers. In Rosenthal, D., and Kety, S.S. (Eds.): *The Transmission of Schizophrenia.*

Elmsford, N.Y., Pergamon Press, 1968.

28. Meehl, P.E.: High school yearbooks: A reply to Schwarz. *J Abnorm Psychol, 77:*143-147, 1971.

29. Michael, C.M., Morris, D.P., and Soroker, E.: Follow-up studies of shy, withdrawn children. II. Relative incidence of schizophrenia. *Am J Orthopsychiatry, 27:*331-337, 1957.

30. Morris, D.P., Soroker, E., and Burrus, G.: Follow-up studies of shy, withdrawn children. I. Evaluation. *Am J Orthopsychiatry, 24:*743-754, 1954.

31. Neale, J.M. and Cromwell, R.L.: Attention and schizophrenia. In Maher, B.A. (Ed.): *Progress in Experimental Personality Research.* New York, Acad Pr, 1970.

32. Neale, J.M. and Weintraub, S.: Children vulnerable to psychopathology: The Stony Brook High-Risk Project. *J Abnorm Child Psychol, 3:*95-113, 1975.

33. Olver, R.R. and Hornsby, J.R.: On equivalence. In Bruner, J.S., Olver, R.R., and Greenfield, P.M. (Eds.): *Studies in Cognitive Growth.* New York, Wiley, 1966.

34. Pekarik, G., Prinz, R.J., Liebert, D.E., Weintraub, S., and Neale, J.M.: A sociometric technique for measuring children's social behavior. *J Abnorm Child Psychol, 4:*83-97, 1976.

35. Phillips, L.: *Human Adaptation and Its Failures.* New York, Acad Pr, 1968.

36. Pollack, M., Woerner, M.G., Goodman, W., and Greenberg, I.M.: Childhood development patterns of hospitalized adult schizophrenics and non-schizophrenic patients and their siblings. *Am J Orthopsychiatry, 36:*510-517, 1966.

37. Rapoport, A.: *Two Person Game Theory.* Ann Arbor, U of Mich Pr, 1966.

38. Roff, M.: *Some Developmental Aspects of Schizoid Personality.* Report No. 65-4, U.S. Army Medical Research and Development Command, March, 1965.

39. Roff, M. and Sells, S.B.: Juvenile delinquency in relation to peer acceptance-rejection and socioeconomic status. *Psychol Schools, 5:*3-18, 1968.

40. Schaefer, E.S.: Children's reports of parental behavior: An inventory. *Child Dev, 36:*413-434, 1965.

41. Sells, S.B., Roff, M., Cox, S.H., and Mayer, M.: *Peer Acceptance-rejection and Personality Development.* Final report of Project OE 5-0417, Contract OE 2-10-051, Office of Education, January, 1967.

42. Silverman, J.: The problem of attention in research and theory in schizophrenia. *Psychol Rev, 71:*383-393, 1964.

43. Smith, G.: Usefulness of peer ratings of personality in educational research. *Educ Psychol Measurement, 24:*967-984, 1967.

44. Spitzer, R. and Endicott, J.: *Current and Past Psychopathology Scales (CAPPS).* New York, Evaluations Unit, Biometrics Research, New York State Department of Mental Hygiene, 1968.

45. Spitzer, R., Gibbon, M., and Endicott, J.: *Family Evaluation Form.* New York, Evaluations Unit, Biometrics Research, New York State Department of Mental Hygiene, 1971.

46. Spivack, G. and Spotts, J.: *The Devereux Child Behavior Rating Scale Manual.* Devon, Pennsylvania, The Devereux Foundation, 1966.

47. Spivack, G., and Swift, M.: *Devereux Elementary School Behavior Rating Scale Manual.* Devon, Pennsylvania, The Devereux Foundation, 1967.

48. Spivack, G., Swift, M., and Prewitt, J.: Syndromes of disturbed classroom behavior: A behavioral diagnostic system for elementary schools. *J Special Educ, 5:*269-292, 1972.

49. Stennet, R.G.: Emotional handicap in the elementary school years: Phase or disease? *Am J Orthopsychiatry, 36:*444-449, 1966.

50. Teele, J.E., Schleifer, M.J., Corman, L., and Larson, K.: Teacher ratings, sociometric status, and choice reciprocity of antisocial and normal boys. *Group Psychother, 19:*183-192, 1966.

51. Tutko, T.A. and Spence, J.T.: The performance of process and reactive schizophrenics and brain injured subjects on a conceptual task. *J Abnorm Soc Psychol, 65:*387-394, 1962.

52. Venables, P.: Input dysfunction in schizophrenia. In Maher, B.A. (Ed.): *Progress in Experimental Personality Research.* New York, Acad Pr, 1964.

53. Waring, M., and Ricks, D.F.: Family patterns of children who became adult schizophrenics. *J Nerv Ment Dis, 140:*351-364, 1965.

54. Weintraub, S. A., Margolies, P., and Neale, J.M.: Schizophrenic patients and their spouses as parents: Their children's perceptions. Unsubmitted manuscript, SUNY at Stony Brook, 1976.

55. Weintraub, S.A., Neale, J.M., and Liebert, D.E.: Teacher ratings of children vulnerable to psychopathology. *Am J Orthopsychiatry, 45:* 838-845, 1975.

56. Wiggins, J.S. and Winder, C.L.: The peer nomination inventory: An empirically derived sociometric measure of adjustment in pre-adolescent boys. *Psychol Rep, 9:*643-677, 1969.

57. Wittman, M.P.: Diagnostic and prognostic significance of the shut-in personality type as a prodromal factor in schizophrenia. *J Clin Psychol, 4:*211-214, 1958.

CHAPTER 8.

MEGAVITAMINS AND DIET

W. D. HITCHINGS, M.D.

IT HAS been said that megavitamins have no place in the treatment of children who are mentally disturbed. My experience has been to the contrary and so I beg to differ.

During the last year of my training as a fellow in child psychiatry, I was working with a very disturbed child. He had not improved with "play therapy" and was being considered for institutional care. Someone outside the clinic had read that megavitamins had been used in Canada for the treatment of emotionally disturbed adults. These vitamins were also being used in the United States for emotionally disturbed children, but in a very limited fashion. It was requested that I try this treatment, and I agreed to do so.

A six-year-old boy was the first in a long series of very disturbed people to be treated with megavitamins, minerals, and diet. The patient is now in his second year of college. For a number of years, he had been full of psychoses.

Briefly, the treatment consists in giving huge doses of water-soluble vitamins and "new vitamins" daily. Specifically, the vitamins I use for children are vitamin C (1000 mg daily), vitamin B_3 (1000 mg daily), vitamin B_6 (250 mg/day) and calcium pantothenate (250 mg/day).

The use of trace minerals varies from one patient to another. They are prescribed on the basis of the results obtained from "hair analysis." Minerals are normally in the body, but an attempt is made to lower those that are at above normal levels and to elevate those that are too low. A number of minerals are found as contaminants in the body, and when found at elevated levels, they act as toxins. One of these commonly found in children in large cities is lead. Mercury, nickel, and cadmium could also be poisoning agents. Trace minerals, such as copper and potassium, can also act as toxins if they are highly elevated.

A further facet of treatment is the use of a high-protein, low-carbohydrate diet. Refined sugars and flours have had all minerals and vitamins removed in the processing. It is highly questionable, as well as controversial, how valuable food is after being processed. Processed foods serve as a ready source of refined carbohydrates. It is always well to remind ourselves that allegedly we are now eating 125 pounds of sugar a year, whereas 100 years ago, the intake was no more than 4 or 5 pounds per year. Again and again, when the emotionally disturbed child first comes for treatment, he is on large amounts of refined sugar. Reducing the amount or eliminating the refined sugar altogether from the diet, will frequently, in itself, reduce a great deal of the hyperactivity that is seen so commonly in this child.

One may justly raise the question, that if we do not know specifically how the vitamins the megadoses achieve the results that they do, is there any logical reason for giving them at all? Doctor Linus Pauling has pointed out how the phenomenon of general anesthesia illustrates the dependence of the mind on its molecular environment. Those of us living through the 1960s and early 1970s of this century are well aware of the profound effects exerted on the mind by such substances as LSD, mescaline, and others. Pauling further points out that the proper functioning of the mind is known to require the presence of molecules of many different substances in the brain. For example, "Mental disease can result from a low concentration of the following vitamins in the brain: thiamine (B_1), nicotinic acid (B_3), pyridoxine (B_6), cyanocobalamin (B_{12}), biotin (H), ascorbic acid (C), and folic acid.

There is evidence that mental functioning and behavior are also affected by changes in the concentration of substances that are normally present in the brain. These are glutamic acid, uric acid and aminobutyric acid." (Pauling)

Furthermore, many investigators have pointed out that "schizophrenic" patients show an increased rate of metabolism of vitamin C. In the southern states of the United States many people suffered from an illness known as *pellagra* for many years. Some of the most distressing symptoms in this illness are those of a psychosis. My patients were given nicotinamide (vitamin B_3), and the psychotic symptoms disappeared. All the above facts have been known for several years by many medical practitioners. It seems strange indeed that, when psychotic symptoms have been permanently relieved by a specific vitamin or combination of vitamins, these therapeutic agents would not also be tried in the treatment of schizophrenia — one of the most potent producers of psychoses both in the child and the adult. Furthermore, children who suffer from schizophrenia also have great difficulty in learning.

In some cases, the improvement of children with learning difficulties associated with schizophrenia seems quite miraculous. During the past four years, I examined a very disturbed child who at three years of age had no speech development. He was extremely hyperactive and had developed no control of bowel or bladder function. He would eat dirt from the floor and consume fecal material. The patient also had a very high level of lead as determined by hair analysis. A few months later, after starting a vitamin and mineral treatment and a high-protein, low-carbo-hydrate diet, the patient developed speech. He soon gained control of his bowel and bladder, and the hyperactivity slowly decreased. When the child was five years of age, he underwent an extensive examination by the educational authorities. They were unable to detect any mental abnormality at that time. He was placed in a normal kindergarten class and he did well.

The majority of patients do not recover as quickly as the disturbed patient mentioned. In the case of children, I feel that we can expect them in treatment through adolescence and high school. There are many ups and downs, hills and valleys on the road to recovery. However, in spite of this, there is a continuous and slow progress back to normality.

We are frequently told, especially by people who have not used the above method, that large doses of vitamins are toxic and will result in injury to the patient. In my experience, I have not found this to be true. On the contrary, based on my past experience and in view of the results obtained, the use of megavitamins, minerals, and diet have been beneficial in the treatment of children suffering from autism, schizophrenia, and brain damage and learning disabilities that may arise as a result of these disorders.

CHAPTER 9.

TEACHING PARENTS TO TEACH THEIR CHILDREN:

The Behavior Modification Approach

KENNETH F. KAUFMAN, Ph.D.

I AM GOING to discuss the development of training programs for parents of autistic children at Sagamore Children's Center.

I began my association with parents of autistic children four years ago. While working as a ward psychologist at Sagamore Children's Center, the state psychiatric hospital for children on Long Island, I received a request from a large, private, nonprofit school serving autistic children to act as a classroom consultant to the teachers. I was struck with the amount of dedication and skill that seemed necessary to deal with three to six of these frequently bizarre and forbidding children six hours a day, five days a week.

Despite my previous experience as a behavior modifier, I felt unprepared for this particular consulting role. I had little to offer them other than rather standard behavior mod reminders that the teachers should exercise more care in reinforcement selection and delivery or that they might be inadvertently maintaining some of the bizarre behaviors that they were complaining about by attending to them.

There was one area that I found particularly perturbing to me when dealing with the teachers. Too frequently, I heard disparaging remarks about the parents of these children. I was not sure whether these statements stemmed from a theoretical bias against parents of children with autism (in a Bettelheim sense) or whether the comments originated from things that some parents had actually done. The teachers' complaints usually con-

96

cerned something as innocuous as an inappropriate lunch or snack brought to school by a child or perhaps the failure of the mother to dress the child with an extra sweater on a windy day. As I listened to the teachers, I could not keep myself from feeling sorry for these parents — who, if nothing else, were never present to defend themselves. It occurred to me that the job of raising an autistic child must be incredibly difficult, a job for which no parent could possibly have been prepared. Can you imagine, I wondered to myself, what it would be like to live with a child like this and still maintain a normal household, or even more, one's sanity? But it appeared that few teachers had an appreciation for this, or so it seemed.

My concern for the plight of parents had begun to blossom one year prior to this. My position at Sagamore had led me into the design of ward token economy programs for delinquent-type, behavior-disordered children. Such programs had been extremely helpful for the inhospital management and habilitation of these youngsters, yet I had found that many of them reverted to deviant behaviors when they returned home to that old environment which had shaped the behavior problems in the first place. In 1971, I had begun organized parent education classes at Sagamore using a behavior modification approach[4] in an effort to stimulate generalization of inpatient gains. These programs were extended to serve outpatients in 1974, and since then, over 750 families of behavior disordered, hyperactive, learning-disabled, etc., children and adolescents have been involved in instructional programs in Sagamore's Behavior Management Unit, the parent education division at the Center. Working with parents of children from a school such as this, therefore, was a natural extension of my interest in parent programs.

In the fall of 1972, I decided, with the permission of the school officials, to begin to meet with some parents of autistic children. It is interesting to note that I had certain misconceptions of that group. For one thing, I had the mistaken expectation (perhaps it was "reaction formation" to my experience with the teachers) that these parents would be a super-competent group, knowledgeable about behavioral principles, autism, and their interrelationships. (In retrospect, this impression probably came from the efforts of one family who had participated in individual behavioral parent training at Sagamore and had some remarkable success. Portions of this work had been documented and publicized[5,6] and will be touched upon later.) But, of course, my expectations were not confirmed. At a series of "rap sessions," I found a group of parents that were floundering, at best. They had few hard facts about their children's condition, no formal knowledge of behavioral principles, and most strikingly, a disdain for professionals that rivaled that the teachers had expressed toward parents. Their target was not the teachers, however, who were perceived, by and large, as caring and skillful. But, they were quite expressive about psychologists, psychiatrists, social workers, pediatricians, and neurologists. It was almost obsessional how parents would document the callousness, the misdiagnoses, and the general lack of concern of many of the mental health professionals with whom they had dealt in the past. But, as I listened, I realized that these parents were frustrated over the professionals' inability to solve the puzzling mysteries of their children's behavior. Of course, many of them were told that their children would "grow out of it." To the parent of the autistic child, there was a constant feeling that professionals really did not care. If they did, it was argued, they would help.

In defense of the professionals, most of the language-delayed children seen at two to three years of age do improve. But for the parent of the severely impaired, mute autistic, the prediction of the developmental lag being overcome was clearly wrong. (I could find less to forgive in the behavior of the professionals who asked the probing questions designed to uncover the source of the "refrigerant" responsible for their child's autism or of the professionals who suggested psychotherapeutic treatment for the parents, sometimes at the expense of education of the child, even when the diagnosis of autism had been confirmed.)

The rap groups led me to realize that the best kind of help for the parent of the autistic child was the kind that provided relief — relief from the destruction, self-stimulation, lack of communication, lack of toilet training, relief from the pitiful puzzle that autism presents. Certainly empathy and reflection were useful

for these parents, but it was clear that it was not enough.   It
seemed logical that what the parents needed was practical help.
After all, the teachers had been able to survive in school because
they had learned to structure their students' days, to offer them
activities to engage in, and to reward them when they functioned
according to task demands.   But the teachers had been prepared
to do their job by a myriad of special education courses, practicum,
and hours of on-the-job supervision.   No one could expect that
parents of autistic children would enroll in master's degree programs.   Even if they did, was it reasonable or even wise for parents to change their households in to classrooms?   Of course, the
answer was no, but a qualified no.   It was clear that of all those
people who had contact with autistic children, the teachers fared
best.   It was from that group from which the parents and I had to
learn.   And it was from the principles of behavior modification
that we had to borrow if we were going to help the parents of
autistic children.

In the spring of 1973, the first behavior modification course on
Long Island for parents of autistic children was organized.   A
total of sixty-two parents and siblings attended this nine-session
course.   The class format included lectures and discussions based
upon Luke Watson's *Child Behavior Modification* text.[18]   Topics
covered included the differences between autistic and normal
children, the nature of "psychoeducational" treatment of autistic
children, but more importantly, basic operant learning principles including reinforcement, shaping, stimulus control, punish-
ment, and extinction, etc.   Parents were taught the elementary techniques for data collection and urged to become actively
involved applying the behavior modification techniques and
principles, using their data to evaluate the success of their efforts.
In order to facilitate practical applications, illustrative films were
shown, including the Lovaas segment of *Reinforcement Therapy;** *Teaching the Mentally Retarded Child — A Positive Approach;†* and *Genesis, Ask Just For Little Things,* and *I'll
Promise You a Tomorrow.‡*

---

*Distributed by Smith, Kline and French.
† By Bensberg and Colwell, distributed by NIMH.
‡The Step-Behind Series, distributed by Hallmark Films and Recordings, Balti-
more, Maryland.

Classroom meetings began with a quiz using short, objective questions taken from the exercises and assignments from Waston's book. Both correct and incorrect answers were then discussed, which provided a review of reading assignments. Parents were encouraged to raise questions when they seemed relevant, although care had to be taken to insure that not too much time was being spent on a single child's problem. Quizzes were graded by exchanging papers or self-checking, but no contingencies were applied for high or low scores. The remainder of the class time was spent in discussion of specific and general examples of how parents had or could have applied behavior modification principles effectively to manage their children at home. Every effort was made to make the parents feel comfortable with their children, yet emphasizing that any situation, no matter how difficult, could be made more tolerable if they, the parents, actively intervened, using behavioral principles to encourage more appropriate behaviors and discourage inappropriate ones.

To say the least, this course was very well received by parents. Despite its obvious shortcomings (to be discussed later) it provided for many parents, the first practical alternative to the "Do nothing — Accept-your-child-for-what-he-is" advice that had too often been given in the past. All along, parents had been asking for something else to do, and they were grateful for a course which gave them some alternative. Comments such as the following one taken from a parent's evaluation of the course were typical:

> The very fact that this course took place was the answer to a long-term need. I only wish that we could have had the benefit of this course four years ago when we were so perplexed as to how to handle problem behavior. The course has been a tremendous asset in that it has given us an awareness of how our responses reinforce behavior. We feel much more confident in approaching behavior problems and in teaching new behavior.

Two other courses following that initial attempt were offered during 1973 to 1974. Curricula were similar although some changes were made. The Watson text supplemented by films was used and classes still followed the quiz-lecture-discussion format. The first change was a stronger emphasis on data collection. I had attended a two-day workshop given by Ogden Lindsley at the 1973 Annual Meeting and Convention of the National Society for Autistic Children in St. Louis, Missouri. That workshop showed convincingly that charting children's behavior on the Standard Behavior Chart could be a useful tool in evaluating their progress. I acquired the appropriate materials and attempted to duplicate Doctor Lindsley's rather entertaining workshop for the thirty-five parent participants in a course offered in the fall of 1973. Parents were clearly intrigued by Lindsley's methods, and a few even mastered them. All were fascinated by the wrist counters they received, and almost everyone did some counting and charting even if it was not of the Lindsley variety. (For a review of precision teaching methods, see Kunzelman.[11])

A second modification in these next two courses involved the addition of a parent presentation to the course curriculum. In November of 1973, Mr. and Mrs. H. offered a live demonstration of the training sessions they had developed for their son, whose progress had been impressive after they had been trained in behavior modification techniques.[5]

At the age of seven, in 1970, a mute, destructive, untoilet-trained, and generally unsocialized autistic child was brought to Sagamore. Three years later, after an active intervention program that included an appropriate school placement, a program of respite services at Sagamore (weekdays at home and weekends at the hospital), and daily twenty-minute, parent-conducted inhome educational sessions, this child was fully toilet trained, no longer destructive at home, following directions and requests, using approximately sixty spoken words appropriately and beginning to tolerate and even seek affection from others.[6] A complete summary of this youngster's progress is found in Table 9-1.

When Mr. H. described the progress of his son and later when Mrs. H. gave a "live demonstration" of training sessions with their son from behind a one-way mirror, those parents who observed this had one of two reactions. Some parents felt put off, saying, "These parents must be special people. This child must be different from mine. I can't possibly do that." Others said, "I can do that too! That's a real family that I can identify with. How do I begin?" For that latter group, the demonstration provided an inspirational model, and they went home resolving to do as Mr. and Mrs. H. had done — they were going to get involved in the education of their autistic child. Many did; approximately one half of the enrollees in the fall of 1973 workshop were doing some systematic teaching of their child by the time the course had ended.

TABLE 9-I

PROGRESS OF AN AUTISTIC CHILD FOLLOWING PARENT EDUCATION, APPROPRIATE EDUCATION PROGRAMMING, AND RESPITE SERVICES*

Infancy Through Age 4	*Pretreatment Behavior (Age 7)*	*Post-treatment Behavior (Age 10)*
• did not want to be held, preferred bottle to be propped	• smeared feces on wall and self	• fully bowel and urine trained, day and night
• seldom cried	• had to be locked in bedroom at night	
• unresponsive to normally attention-getting sounds	• made loud yelping noises	• no lock required
• stiff when carried	• ripped clothing, blanket, curtains, and shades before going to sleep at night	• ripping of clothing, etc. has stopped
• unaware of surroundings, wanted to be only in his bedroom or kitchen		• can be trusted to look at books and magazines for short periods without ripping
• rocked on all fours	• wet self twenty or more times per day, soiled self at least two times per day	
• no eye contact		
• never crawled, moved across floor in sitting position	• ripped magazines and papers	• uses approximately sixty words
• did not walk until nineteen months, except in crib or playpen	• peeled paint and wallpaper off walls, if left to himself	• can identify about seventy-five additional words and match to picture
• refused table food until three one-half years old		
• insensitivity to pain	• no speech	• spontaneous speech developing — makes requests for object,
• failure to play	• followed no directions or commands, no understanding of language;	
• no speech development		

TABLE 9-I (Continued)

Infancy Through Age 4	Pretreatment Behavior (Age 7)	Post-treatment Behavior (Age 10)
• preservation/ sameness	relied on visual clues • no purposeful play or activity • extreme hyperactivity, required constant, total supervision	food, etc.; says "hello, goodbye, I see —" appropriate other phrases too • follows some simple directions and commands, much more understanding of language; does not rely as much on visual clues • learned to tie shoes • plays more appropriately • sets table for dinner • watches education T.V. programs intently with apparent interest • off medication since November, 1974

*From K.F. Kaufman, E. Alexander, P. Alexander, and C. Hansen, and D Hansen, *Parent Education and Rehabilitation*. Presented at the First New York State Conference on Comprehensive Rehabilitation, Monticello, New York, April, 1975. Courtesy of K.F. Kaufman.

By the spring of 1974, a third parent group had been assembled, this time at Sagamore. For the first time parents with no other connection with the Center were invited to join a Sagamore-sponsored parent-training group. It was becoming clear that the real target group of parents to be reached were the parents of younger, more recently diagnosed autistic children. Twelve parents with children from nine different special school programs enrolled in this program. (This provides an indication that news of parent training program had spread rapidly across Long Island.)   This ten-session workshop retained almost the identical format to the two previous courses.

But by this time, the goal of our program was becoming clearer.   Parents were expected to begin some type of daily training program with their child.   Parents were told that good behavioral training sessions would provide the learning laboratory for them to develop the confidence to manage their children more successfully.   To emphasize this point, Mrs. A., a participant in the previous course, made a presentation to this group of parents midway through the program.   Videotapes of some of the training sessions that she and her husband had been conducting with their five-and-one-half-year-old autistic son were used to illustrate Mrs. A.'s presentation.

Most of the sessions involved speech and language training. The training techniques utilized were based on principles learned at the fall, 1973 workshop combined with those acquired through Mrs. A.'s observations of her son's behaviorally oriented language therapy.   Parents who attended this demonstration had reactions similar to those who had seen the parent demonstration during the fall course.   They seemed inspired more by watching and talking to other parents involved in training than by books or films.   Following this talk, every parent began a project; some chose toilet training, others self-help skills, and a few tried their hand at language shaping.   All of them reported finding their children easier to manage, attributing their success to the skills learned in teaching sessions.   Finally, it appeared that we were on our way to finding a successful formula to educating parents of autistic children.

The summer of 1974 was a time of reflection and planning. Sagamore had applied for and had been awarded a Hospital Improvement Grant (#02-R000,023) from NIMH to develop outpatient services.   A portion of that funding was requested to support more intensive efforts to develop our educational programs for autistic children. Once funding appeared certain, we tried to assess what we had learned in conducting the three previous parent-training classes. This could be summarized as follows:

1. Parents welcomed the opportunity to participate in organized classes designed to teach them behavioral principles. They enjoyed the lecture-discussion-film-quiz-format — preferring structured sessions to open-ended rap groups.
2. Parents had some difficulty learning to record and chart behavior, but many would do so when data collection was shown to have some practical utility.
3. Parents were most impressed and motivated by seeing other parents like themselves engage in training their own children. Such demonstrations were effective for those who were unconvinced by books and films alone.
4. Parents who actually ran training sessions with their children regularly, no matter how brief and regardless of what they were training, gained more confidence in their ability to manage their children than those who did not do any training.
5. Parents had considerable difficulty deciding what to teach their children. Not being educators, they seemed unable to determine what was important for their children to learn next. Once they made their decision about what skills to teach, they frequently had difficulty figuring out how to teach it.
6. Parents seemed to want more individualized inhome help with their training sessions, once they had learned behavioral principles in classes.
7. Finally, despite all of our positive impressions, we had not scientifically documented, nor could we find adequate documentation in the literature, that this or any other type of training program for parents of autistic children led to skill or attitude change on the part of the parents or their children.

During the summer of 1974, the search to improve our parent

education programs led us to the work of Doctor Martin A. Kozloff. In his book, *Reaching the Autistic Child: A Parent Training Program*,[10] he described an extensive program to train parents of autistic and severely behaviorally disordered children which he had developed while working at Washington University in St. Louis and extended to families in Boston, Massachusetts. In a memorable visit, our staff traveled to see Kozloff at Boston University in August 1974. Kozloff graciously offered us the preprints of his more recent book, which seemed to be perfect for our needs. This volume, *Educating Children with Learning and Behavior Problems*,[9] derived from his experiences, consisted of the complete assessment and training curriculum used by parents in his previous work. It consists of four major components, including the following:

1. A thorough explanation of the reinforcement principles necessary to conduct behavioral skill training sessions.
2. A detailed assessment system, the *Behavior Evaluation Scale* (BES), which enables parents to pinpoint their child's strengths and weaknesses in six major skill areas, as well as in the realm of problem behaviors; skills are developmentally sequenced, that is, elementary skills requisite to the development of more complex behaviors are clearly indicated.
3. Several explicitly written chapters describing how one can design a teaching session on any skill listed in the BES, indexed on a page-by-page basis. Complete instructions on setting up a home training program are included from data collection procedures to precise information on proper selection and sequencing of behaviors to be trained.
4. A discussion of how to deal with problem behaviors both within and outside of teaching sessions.

In addition to supplying this outstanding curriculum, Kozloff provided us with minutes of his parent-training class and details of inhome tutoring sessions conducted with each family in order to help us to replicate his procedures at Sagamore. In the winter of 1974-75, we were ready to begin.

Our first step was to contact two local schools that served autistic children to ask them to refer to us intact mother-father families with young (six years old or less) autistic children. Following an intensive interview, eleven of these families decided to enroll in our inhome training program. Our interviewing techniques were based upon those Kozloff had used. He had attempted to screen families, choosing those who were most motivated. At the interview, families were told what would be involved in our program and given a choice as to whether they wanted to be included. Some families indicated that schedule demands prevented them from participating. Others felt that a program such as ours was too demanding. Of the eleven families who wanted to participate, three families said they were willing to enter a materials-alone treatment group (described later). Another family was randomly chosen for the materials-alone group. Thus, seven families remained. They were assigned to our comprehensive treatment group, which will be discussed in detail below.

The Comprehensive Training Program for families of autistic children had four major components. I will describe each briefly and explain its relationship to the program. A complete week-by-week outline of the Comprehensive Training Program is found in Table 9-II.

DEPOSIT CONTRACTS: Learning to conduct training sessions with one's own autistic child is hard work, requiring a great deal of effort on the part of both the parents and the staff that trains them. The deposit contract system ensures that both staff and parents fulfill their obligations to the program even though a particular task may be distasteful to them. Before any training was begun, both parents and staff signed a detailed agreement outlining their respective responsibilities throughout the program. Parents agreed to attend scheduled meetings, do assigned homework, prepare for home visits, and conduct daily training sessions with their child. Staff members agreed to prepare for and be on time for class and home visits, to provide necessary materials to families, etc. To back up the contract, both parents *and* staff placed three certified checks in the amounts of 10/10,000, 15/

TABLE 9-II
OUTLINE OF COMPREHENSIVE TRAINING PROGRAM

Week 1 *Class 1*
Overview of training program
Overview of behavorial approach
Review of deposit contracts
Discuss Behavior Evaluation
   Scale
Show and Discuss Lovaas Film
Assignment: Read Kozloff, 1974,
Chapters 1, 2[9]

Week 2 *Class 2*
Review Chapter 1
Discuss concepts, such as what
is behavior, reinforcement, pun-
ishment, antecedents-consequents
Discuss importance of measure-
ment
Assignment: Read Chapter 3[9]

Week 3 *Class 3*
Review of Chapter 3
Discuss rewards, primary and
   learned, social and activity,
   schedules, etc.
Discuss chaining
Show baseline videos that dem-
   onstrate parents' use of re-
   wards, praise, etc.
Discuss physical environment
   best for training
Each family meets with home-
   trainer to go over homework
Assignment: Chapter 4[9]

Week 4 *Class 4*
Review Chapter 4[9]
Discuss educational and teaching
   programs
Review Kozloff's Skill Sequences
   and Behavior Evaluation Table
Discuss focus on training skill as
   opposed to working on "behavior problem"
Hometrainers review each family's BES and BET
Assignment: Read Chapter 5[9]
   and plan to take baseline data

Week 5 *Home Visit 1*
Class 5
Review Chapter 5[9]

Discuss relationship between program and children's schools
Discuss importance of measurement — pinpointing, counting,
   charting
Review strategies in using BES
Discuss importance of beginning
   with most basic skills: eye contact, cooperation with simple
   requests, sitting and working.
Observe videos and practice
   selecting and defining targets
Assignment: Read Chapter 6[9]

Week 6 *Home Visit 2*
Class 6
Discuss Chapter 6[9], using model
   and role-play techniques to
   demonstrate important aspects
   of running teaching session
Discuss the role of environment
   in creating teaching atmosphere
Review exact procedures necessary for delivering rewards
   and reinforcers
Discuss shaping, prompting, emphasizing clear signals
Discuss how to handle disruptive
   behavior during teaching sessions
Meet with hometrainers to go
   over baseline data and first
   teaching sessions
Assignment: Read Chapter 7[9]

Week 7 *Home Visit 3*
Class 7
Review Chapter 7 by asking parents to discuss problems they are
   encountering in teaching sessions
Watch videotapes of experienced parents from previous
   programs who have run teaching programs
Assignment: Read Chapter 8[9]

Week 8 *Home Visit 4*
Class 8
Discuss Chapter 8 by having par-

TABLE 9-II — (Continued)

ents working on learning readiness (eye contact, etc.); comment on the teaching programs
Watch and discuss tapes of some parents training pointing out strengths and weaknesses
Assignment: Chapter 9[9]

Week 9 *Home Visit 5*
Class 9
Review material on advanced teaching programs from Chapter 8[9]
Review videos of some parents
Discuss specifics of developing programs for specific skills
One family presents details of this training
Assignment: Read Schreibman and Keogel article from *Psychology Today*[17]

Week 10 *Home Visit 6*
Class 10
Discuss *Psychology Today* article and talk about extent of use of behavioral procedures in Long Island schools for autistics
Review Chapter 10[9] — large motor skills — role play, model, etc. Specific skills in BES
View video of parents working on this skills area
Small-group meetings
Assignment: Chapter 11[9]

Week 11 *Home Visit 7*
Class 11
Discuss the importance of motor imitation
Review techniques for teaching chores and self-help skills
Disscuss feeding problems, toilet training
Parent presentation on cooperation with simple requests, sitting at task, etc.
Assignment: Chapter 12[9]

Week 12 *Home Visit 8*
Class 12
Review Chapter 12

Discuss verbal imitation in detail
Discuss language development outside of teaching sessions
Discuss teaching basic sounds, nonsense syllables
Parent presentations
Group meeting
Assignment: Chapter 13, 14[9]

Week 13 *Home Visit 9*
Class 13
Discuss differences between functional speech and verbal imitation
Review procedures in teaching use of "action" words
Parent presentations
View follow-up tapes of families previously involved in similar programs
Assigned: Chapter 15[9]

Week 14 *Home Visit 10*

Week 15 *Home Visit 11*
Class 14
Discuss prognosis for autistic children
Review schedule for fading regular contacts
Review material on behavior problems and some basic principles of successful behavior management
Parent presentations
Group meetings

Week 16 *Home Visit 12*

Week 17 *Home Visit 13*

Week 18 *Class 15*
Review each parent's progress in training and observe general videotapes
Returned deposit contract money

Summer — Monthly phone calls and home-visits

Follow-up meetings monthly with format involving review of each parent's progress and problems in training and managing children. Monthly home visits.

10,000, and 20/10,000 of their annual income in a locked vault. Checks were required to be made out to an organization which the individual does *not* like (their so-called "least favorite charity"). It was agreed that failure to live up to one's contract would result in checks being mailed immediately.

The deposit contract was a very effective tool. It clearly indicated that we meant business and that we expected parents to work hard. It was important that the staff take the contract seriously, thereby insuring that the parents would complete difficult assignments which if not performed might have been a barrier to effective training management of their child.

CURRICULUM: Kozloff's book, *Educating Children With Learning and Behavior Problems*,[9] was used as the primary curriculum source. Parents were able to select behaviors and plan teaching sessions using the Behavior Evaluation Scale. Once these programs were outlined, they were able to consult appropriate chapters for guidance on specific techniques necessary to teach particular skills. In our comprehensively trained group, material concerning teaching strategies and techniques were reviewed and emphasized during classes and home visits. Some other reading material,[17] films, e.g. Lovaas segment of the *Reinforcement Therapy* film, and videotapes[6] were used as supplements to Kozloff's book, but Kozloff[9] was clearly the major source of information for the parents.

CLASSES: A working knowledge of behavioral principles, as well as considerable information concerning teaching techniques, was required before parents could effectively set up a training program for their child. We had already learned that parents enjoyed and benefitted a great deal from group instruction. In this program, classes consisted largely of lectures and discussions of the material presented in the Kozloff text. This was supplemented by modeling and role playing of teaching sessions early in the program, while later on, parents themselves made presentations of their individual teaching sessions to the rest of the group. They were encouraged to bring in graphs of their data and to comment on their own strengths and weaknesses as trainers as they presented videotapes of home teaching sessions.

There were fifteen classes during the training program. They ranged in length from two to four hours. While much of the content of the class was rather formal, there was usually time for informal discussions about autism and the prognosis of the children. This was encouraged, although care was taken to make certain that parents did not get away from the task at hand — learning to teach their children.

Following large-group sessions, shorter small-group meetings were held with each staff member meeting with those two or three families with whom they conducted home training. These meetings allowed for discussion of more specific problems and for setting up appointments for home visits.

HOME VISITS: A most important aspect of the program was individual home visits made by project staff to the homes of families in the program. The purpose of these visits was to help individualize programs for each family and to provide feedback to the parents on the strengths and weaknesses of their training skills. A typical home visit included a brief discussion of the previous week's training session with the child and a demonstration of a training session by both the mother and father of the training that each was presently conducting. The home trainer would then coach parents, providing feedback, modeling, and reinforcement for the parent, depending upon the quality of the teaching session. Monthly videotapes of training sessions were carried out during this time. These tapes were reviewed immediately at home so that the trainers could provide the most graphic illustrations of parents' strengths and weaknesses as trainers. Of course, all of this information was used to plan future teaching sessions. Home visits also provided a chance for staff to discuss particular problems and concerns by families. The home trainer often served as counselor, a friend, and as a shoulder for the parents to lean on, especially toward the end of the program. In some cases, when the program ended, friendly social relationships between the home trainer and the families continued for long periods of time.

There were thirteen home visits lasting one to two hours. These took place weekly beginning during the fifth week of the program and extending until the program's conclusion.

All four components of the Comprehensive Training Program blended together to provide an intensive integrated learning experience for parents, designed to take inexperienced but motivated parents of autistic children and within four months make them competent effective trainers and managers of their youngsters' behavior.

When the Comprehensive Training Program was completed in June 1975, we were satisfied that we had successfully replicated the clinical aspects of Kozloff's parent education program. This was largely a subjective judgment based upon the fact that all of the parents (mothers *and* fathers) seemed confident in their ability to conduct training sessions with their children. We were satisfied that these sessions were being carried out with considerable skill and enthusiasm. Parent reports added considerable weight to our subjective impressions. For example, two of the fathers in our program reported that participation in the training program caused a complete turnabout in the previously hopeless picture they had painted for their youngsters. For most of the parents, the daily work with their children offered them a new appreciation for their autistic children and a greater hope for their future.

The training sessions designed by parents for their children in this program varied widely. Almost every child was deficient in the most basic area outlined by Kozloff, *learning readiness.* Parent-collected baselines generally indicated low levels of eye contact (both spontaneous and requested), as well as poor responsiveness to directions. Educational programs invariably started out, therefore, at these most elementary levels, but quickly progressed to training in more complex skill areas, including looking at objects on request, throwing and catching a ball, identifying colors, imitating sounds, reading letters, identifying objects, using prepositions correctly, and asking appropriate questions, etc. Most parents worked in two or three major skill areas simultaneously, using their training techniques not only in short (fifteen to forty-five minute) formal teaching sessions, but also in the course of routine daily interactions with their children. While no "miracle cures" were apparent, the parents clearly saw their children as more responsible and easier to manage as a function of these efforts.

Of course, not all of the children progressed equally, nor did all parents find the program as easy to apply. Two of the seven children were major management problems before the program began and presented the most difficulty. We chose to ignore these problems at first and to (1) not concentrate on management techniques for this disruptiveness, (2) preferring, instead, to stress the start of teaching sessions.

It soon became obvious that our "accentuate-the-positive" approach was frustrating to families who were constantly facing severe behavior problems, such as destructiveness and extreme hyperactivity. These families were often too exhausted physically and emotionally to maintain teaching sessions. In one case, effective teaching only took place after the child had brief separation from his family, spending two weeks at Sagamore, toward the end of the training program. Following this respite, and then only with a five day at home, two day at the hospital program,[5] did this youngster progress at a good pace. (Future programs need to be keenly sensitive to the individual needs of parents and their children. While a method such as Kozloff's may be a significant benefit to all families with this type of child, a vast network of supportive services may be necessary for such parent education programs to be maximumally effective.)

For the seven comprehensively trained families, the subjective reports appeared to be in our favor. However, as stated earlier, a major dissatisfaction with our previous work and with the field in general had been the lack of objective data that clearly delineated the effect of parent training programs for parents of autistic children. In undertaking this project, our goal had been to move in the direction of a more objective evaluation system for programs of this type. Before discussing the objective evaluation used for the current program, I would like to discuss those variables that should be measured in an *ideal* evaluation system for a training program such as ours. Such a system would need to include measures of change in at least the following areas:

1. The parents' knowledge of behavioral principles
2. The parents' skill as trainers or teachers of their own children
3. The parents' competence as managers of their children's behavior outside training sessions, i.e. during day-to-day nonteaching, related events
4. The parents' attitudes toward their autistic child and their expectancies for the future
5. The parents' attitudes toward each other and toward their nonautistic children
6. The child's intellectual or developmental level compared to children of similar age
7. The child's skills targeted for change during parent conducted teaching sessions
8. The child's skill level changes in other than target areas; i.e. generalization data
9. The child's manageability, i.e. obedience, compliance, responsiveness, etc., during teaching sessions
10. The child's manageability outside of formal teaching sessions
11. The child's performance in nonparent-related environments, such as in school, with peers, etc.

The preceding is probably not a complete list of pre– and postchanges that might be evidenced as a function of a good parent-education program, but there has been little documentation in the literature that any of these changes (except for directly trained within program skills) have taken place. Furthermore, while pre– or postchanges would be encouraging, more long-term evaluations of many years' duration would certainly be necessary to adequately assess the impact of such a parent-education program. It is very possible that short-term gains produced by intensive training programs "wash out" after some time.

Still another vital area of concern may be the selection of appropriate control or comparison groups for the type of investigation. The most obvious answer would be some type of "no treatment" control. But if one suspects that parent training is a critical ingredient to the successful management and treatment of children with autism, then one is faced with the ethical problem of withholding the parent education from a certain percentage of families. This is especially true for the long periods of time required to make the conclusions concerning the efficacy of a particular program. This was the problem we faced before beginning our 1975 program, as we pondered the problem of an adequate control or comparison group for our comprehensively trained parents. A great influence on our choice of such a group came from the work of Bruce Baker and his associates at the Read Project, Harvard University. Because I feel that the Read Project study provides not only an interesting solution to this ethical dilemma but some fascinating results as well, I would like to describe this project in some detail. Baker and his associates had developed a series of nine behaviorally oriented training manuals (four of which have subsequently been published[1]); the target audience was parents of the retarded. These individually bound, 100–page manuals were simply and explicitly written and attractively illustrated. Each covered a different important area relevant to retarded children, such as basic self-help skills, beginning speech, toilet training, play skills, and behavior problems, etc. The manuals were designed to be used independently or in any combination parents wanted, depending upon their youngster's skills or deficits. In a study conducted to assess the effectiveness of the manuals,[2] parents using the manuals alone (with no other professional contact or guidance) were as successful, or in some cases, more successful, in modifying their children's behavior than parents who used the manuals in combination with professionally directed parent groups, home visits by behavioral specialists, or phone calls from project staff.

To us, this impressive finding suggested that excellent materials alone might be the necessary component for an effective parent education program. Furthermore, it was an indication that the proper comparison group for our comprehensively trained group of parents would be a materials-alone group; that is, a group of parents similar in all respects to the parents in the comprehensively trained group, but who received no help from us other than receiving a copy of Kozloff's[9] book. As mentioned earlier, there

were four families in our materials-alone comparison group —
three families who themselves chose to work only with the book
and one family who was selected at random for this type of treatment.

It was hoped that all of the data from the comparison of the
comprehensively trained and materials-alone groups would have
been available for presentation here today, but this data has
only partially been analyzed. A more complete report of this
data should be available at a later date.[8]

Briefly, there were two major variables compared in this study.
The first comparison involved measurement of the parents' development of adequate training skills during teaching sessions.
This was accomplished by the analyses of the videotapes of parent-
conducted training sessions using a specially designed observation
scale[12] that discriminated between appropriate and inappropriate
training behaviors of parents. These included structuring the
environment; obtaining attention, delivery of verbal, physical,
and gestural prompts; as well as material and social reinforcement. Analysis of monthly videotapes showed that both comprehensively treated (Fig. 9-1) and materials-alone (Fig. 9-2) groups
increased the number of appropriate training behaviors and decreased the number of inappropriate teaching behaviors. However, the improvement was significantly greater for the comprehensive group. Figure 9-3 shows that the efficiency ratio (appropriate training behaviors divided by inappropriate training behaviors) for the comprehensive group continued to increase
throughout the program, while leveling off for the parents in the
materials-alone group.

It seems clear from this data that the comprehensively treated
group of parents became more accomplished trainers of their
children than parents using only the Kozloff book[9] alone, although the parents using only the book do, in fact, make some
progress as trainers.

Our second comparison in this study involved changes in skill
level by the children. Of course, we had expected that the superior training ability of the parents in the comprehensive group
would have been reflected in greater skill changes in their chil-

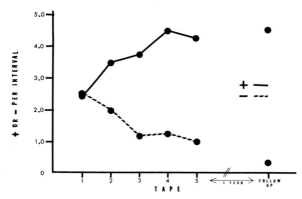

Figure 9-1. Mean number of appropriate (+) and inappropriate (−) teaching behaviors per taped teaching session for parents in the comprehensively trained group. From K.F. Kaufman et al., *Designing and Evaluating Home Educational Programs for the Parents of Autistic Children.* Presented to The Association for the Advancement of Behavior Therapy, New York, New York, 1976. Courtesy of K. F. Kaufman.

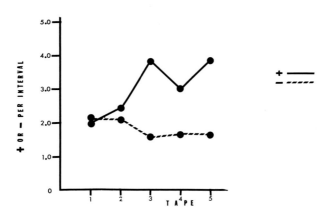

Figure 9-2. Mean number of appropriate (+) and inappropriate (−) teaching behaviors per taped teaching session for parents in the materials-alone group. From K.F. Kaufman et al., *Designing and Evaluating Home Educational Programs for the Parents of Autistic Children.* Presented to The Association for the Advancement of Behavior Therapy, New York, New York, 1976. Courtesy of K.F. Kaufman.

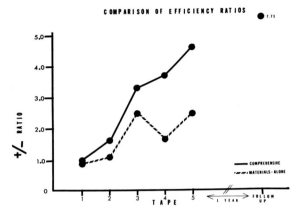

Figure 9-3. Comparison of efficiency ratios (number of appropriate teaching behaviors divided by inappropriate teaching behaviors) calculated for parents in the comprehensively trained and materials-alone groups.   From K.F. Kaufman et al., *Designing and Evaluating Home Educational Programs for the Parents of Autistic Children.* Presented to The Association for the Advancement of Behavior Therapy, New York, New York, 1976. Courtesy of K. F. Kaufman.

dren compared with those of the materials-alone group. In order to measure skill changes, the parent rated Behavior Evaluation Scales were analyzed in a pre– and postprogram comparison. Surprisingly, no differences emerged between the groups on this measure, although there were considerable postprogram improvements for both groups of children. This result is most puzzling and may be reflective of programs with the measure itself, or it may be indicative of too brief a measurement interval to delineate clear differences. If the comprehensively trained group parents are better trainers than materials-alone trainees, skill-change differences in their children may not show up until a longer period of time has passed, i.e. until after many more training sessions are held. Of course, it is possible that no differences in the children will emerge and that, in fact, both groups of youngsters will fare better than those whose parents had not received any training. It is possible, although unlikely, that the changes in the parents will never be reflected in changes in their children.

But this question cannot be answered here, since there was no "no treatment" group for the reasons stated earlier. Further studies, using different experimental designs, such as multiple baselines, are needed to answer these questions.

I have traced the evolutionary trail of Sagamore's educational programs for families with autistic children to its most recent point. I had begun as a consultant to teachers of autistic children and now, four years later, am actively pursuing clinical and research programs designed to help the parents of these children. A great deal of work needs to be done, and some of it has begun. Studies are now being carried out or are being planned to more adequately measure parent-training program effects on the variables described above. These data are tremendously important to the future of autistic children. Until it can be documented that parent education is, in fact, critical to the generalization of educational treatment gains from school to the home and neighborhood environment, parent education will retain its status as a "frill" in schools for the autistic child. It is hoped that our work will demonstrate that parent education is not a "nicety," but a *necessity* in the treatment of autism.

REFERENCES

1. Baker, B.L., Brightman, A.J., Heifetz, L.J., and Murphy, D.M.: *Steps to Independence: A Skill Training Series for Children with Special Needs.* Champaign, Illinois, Res Press, 1976.
2. Baker, B.L., Heifetz, L.J., and Brightman, A.J.: *Parents as Teachers. Manuals for Behavior Modification of the Retarded Child.* Cambridge, Massachusetts, Behavior Education Projects, 1972.
3. Bartak, L. and Rutter, M.: Special education treatment of autistic children. I. Design of study and characteristics of units. *J Child Psychol Psychiatry, 14:*161-179, 1973.
4. Becker, W.: *Parents Are Teachers.* Champaign, Illinois, Res Press, 1971.
5. Drabman, R., Spitalnik, R., Hagamen, M.B., and VanWitsen, B.: The Five-Two Program: An integrated approach to treating severely disturbed children. *Hosp Community Psychiatry, 24:*33-36, 1973.
6. Kaufman, K.F., Alexander, E., Alexander, P., Hansen, C., and Hansen, D.: *Parent Education and Rehabilitation.* Presented at the First New York State Conference on Comprehensive Rehabilitation, Monticello, New York, 1975.
7. Kaufman, K.F. and O'Leary, K.D.: Reward, cost and self-evaluation

procedures for disruptive adolescents in a psychiatric hospital school. *J Appl Behavior Anal, 5:*293-309, 1972.

8. Kaufman, K.F. et al.: *Designing and Evaluating Home Educational Programs for Parents of Autistic Children.* Presented to The Association for the Advancement of Behavior Therapy, New York, New York, 1976.

9. Kozloff, M.A.: *Educating Children with Learning and Behavior Problems.* New York, Wiley, 1974.

10. Kozloff, M.A.: *Reaching the Autistic Child: A Parent Training Program.* Champaign, Illinois, Res Press, 1973.

11. Kunzelman, H. (Ed.): *Precision Teaching.* Seattle, Washington, Special Child Publications, 1970.

12. Liff, W., Casale, F., and Kaufman, K.F.: *The Parent Training Analysis Scale.* Unpublished manuscript. Sagamore Children's Center, Melville, New York, 1975.

13. O'Leary, K.D., Kaufman, K.F., Kass, R., and Drabman, R.: The effects of loud and soft reprimands on the behavior of disruptive students. *Except Child, 37:*145-155, 1970.

14. Rimland, B.: *Infantile Autism.* New York, Appleton, 1964.

15. Rutter, M. and Bartak, L.: Special education treatment of autistic children: A comparative study. Two follow-up findings and implications for services. *J Child Psychol Psychiatry, 14:*241-270, 1973.

16. Santogrossi, D., O'Leary, K.D., Romanczyk, R., and Kaufman, K.F.: Self-evaluation by adolescents in a psychiatric hospital school token program. *J Appl Behavior Anal, 6:*277-287, 1973.

17. Schriebman, L. and Koegel, R.: Autism: A defeatable horror. *Psychol Today, 8:*61-67, 1975.

18. Watson, L.: *Child Behavior Modification: A Manual for Nurses, Teachers and Parents.* Elmsford, New York, Pergamon, 1973.

19. Wing, J. (Ed.): *Early Childhood Autism.* Oxford, England, Pergamon, 1966.

CHAPTER 10.

CLOSING THE PARENT-PROFESSIONAL GAP:
Toward A Better Working Relationship with Parents of Developmentally Disabled Children

BRUCE GROSSMAN, Ph.D.

INTRODUCTION

As a professional psychologist, I have learned a great deal from leading parent groups at the Little Village School, as well as from talking with parents of developmentally disabled children in my clinical practice. To my disappointment, much of the basis for these parents' complaints have to do with their treatment by my fellow professionals. The five most recurring difficulties encountered by parents of developmentally disabled children in their dealing with professionals are discussed:

1. BEING SHUTTLED FROM ONE PROFESSIONAL TO ANOTHER: Very often parents are put to great expense and effort by a referral process that yields very little. While negative findings are sometimes reassuring, the lack of explanation or time offered parents results in confusion and resentment. Parents of the developmentally disabled are often particularly vulnerable, because diagnosis of their children's disabilities is so difficult and, in fact, arbitrary. The experience of being asked to wait hours in a busy hospital for a child to receive a perfunctory examination, with parents given little or no consultation, is all too common.

2. BEING ONLY PARTIALLY INFORMED ABOUT FINDINGS: This brings us to a second common complaint about professionals and their frequent lack of willingness to share information openly with parents. Whether this secretiveness comes from embarrass-

ment or from a professional protectiveness, it is harmful and in most cases unnecessary. As I shall discuss at a later point, parents are the closest to the child's problem and usually the developmentally disabled child's best advocate. Parents need to be informed. Full disclosure should be the motto of the professional, unless otherwise indicated. The informing process is, of course, a delicate one. It requires tact and a gentle educative skill, which should be expected of all professionals, especially those in the mental health professions. Yet it is sorely lacking and parents feel like "busy bodies" trying to dislodge information from professionals, who often give the appearance of being "stone walls."

3. THE LACK OF INTEGRATION BETWEEN PROFESSIONAL EVALUATIONS: This difficulty is clearly related to the earlier two. The movement from professional to professional, each looking at the child from their own vantage point, results in gaps of knowledge which frequently fail to take into account the whole child. The view that each professional has of the child tends to be taken from the vantage point of each one's own particular speciality and, as such, is only a partial view of the child. Too frequently, material gathered in one setting is not available to the professional currently evaluating the child, because of a delay or failure in information sharing. Even more disturbing, information that has been sent from one professional to another is either ignored or disparaged by the second evaluator. When this lack of professional integration of findings exists, it falls to the parents to assume this task, if they can, or to insist on professional help in this process. Accordingly, it is essential that parents be as fully informed as possible by each professional evaluator. In this way, parents will be better able to take a more active role in coordinating information pertinent to decision making about their child.

4. THE LACK OF KNOWLEDGE OF RESOURCES: Again, there is a connection here between this lack of knowledge and other difficulties encountered by parents of developmentally disabled children in their dealings with professionals. While each specialist may be competent in what he or she can observe and do for the child, the applicability and availability of other services are often

not in the specialist's repertoire. This is especially so in the area of remediation and education, but also applies to other services that may require specialized attention for the developmentally disabled. Clearly, knowledge of where all of these services may be found may be beyond the ken of even the best intentioned specialist. On the other hand, there is no excuse for the complete ignorance of the availability of specialized services for the developmentally disabled that abounds in the professional community. In my own experience, some social workers and most schools for these children have the best knowledge of resources.

5. A LACK OF AWARENESS ON THE PART OF PROFESSIONALS OF THE NEEDS OF PARENTS OF THE DEVELOPMENTALLY DISABLED CHILD: Even before Leo Kanner coined the term *refrigerator* mother in 1941, it is likely that parents, as well as professionals, felt there was something wrong with parents, particularly mothers, who produce developmentally disabled children. Inadvertently, looking for an etiology, professionals cast their questions in a form which makes parents prone to guilt even more guilty. While at one point they made parents feel guilty for not institutionalizing their special child, now they are often made to feel guilty if they choose early schooling.

Professionals, who should know better, are too often insensitive to the anxieties, ambivalences, frustrations, and enormous psychological burdens of parents whose children are not following the normal course of development and parents who, rightly or wrongly, are sometimes overprotective, indecisive, and even exasperated. Questionnaires and long interviews are often quite a strain that is sometimes unnecessarily repeated or prolonged. The professional has only to identify the problem, not to accept it and live with it, and that makes a great deal of difference.

THE PSYCHOLOGICAL REACTIONS OF PARENTS WHO LEARN THAT THEIR CHILD HAS AN ABNORMALITY IN DEVELOPMENT

Very much like an initial reaction to the death of a loved one,[4] the parent of the developmentally disabled child often experiences an initial reaction of *denial.* "It's not true; he'll outgrow it," are typical first reactions. Even early identifications can be wrong and are difficult to accept, although acceptance seems to be easier when the child is younger. In many cases one parent, usually the father, is the one to deny the problem, while the other parent has to overcome his/her own anxieties, as well as the spouse's resistance to professional consultation. Denial by one or both parents may be compounded by the reactions of grandparents or even by the pediatrician who frequently echoes the panacea, "let's wait a few months" and continues to write "normal baby" on the chart.

Once the fact that a problem in development exists is admitted, then parents often have to deal with *guilt*. "What did I (we) do wrong?" is the frequent question. A careful look at the prenatal behavior of the mother may reveal some slight misbehavior, (overeating, a fall, too much exercise, too little exercise, etc.) , which may seemingly explain the abnormality but which is often not the actual cause. What about genetics? Very often each side of the family tree is examined, which may be a devisive and guilt-arousing experience. Then there are irregularities in the birth process itself, which may account for the difficulty, but is also a great source of guilt.

Following the assumption of personal blame and the related feeling of guilt, parents often search for an outside target upon which to *project the blame* for the condition of their child. The obstetrician may be blamed for faulty prenatal care and for delivery. The pediatrician may be blamed for a lack of appropriate service. All of these complaints may be justified, but they frequently serve as discharges of tension, which are not as constructive as they are relieving.

Anger in general is a frequent follow-up to the projection of blame. "Why me?" is a question that eventually takes the form of resenting others who have normal children or all those who do not understand, stare, or ask too many questions, etc.

Finally, there is the stage of *acceptance* when parents finally learn to live with all of the feelings mentioned earlier. Yes, the tendency to deny, feel guilty, angry, and resentful are all still there, but they are mostly under control. That comes about when by themselves, or with professional help, parents realize that they may be feeling more sorry for themselves than for their child. They come to realize that their child can be helped and that his or her development does proceed, albeit slowly. They learn that a definition of the success of their developmentally disabled child is relative, but nonetheless significant and a source of happiness for the child and themselves, as long as they accept the disability. As the social psychologist, J.D. Frank[1] demonstrated, even the most objectively successful person can feel like a failure if his "level of aspiration" exceeds his level of achievement.

Of course, all parents of developmentally disabled children do not go through the above-mentioned reactions in the same order or to the same extent. Some stages may not appear at all, although I would submit they happen, if even unconsciously. The nature of parental reaction to a child's developmental disability is dependent on the nature of the disability, which is in turn related to the severity and time of discovery, etc. A parent who learns from the time of a child's birth of a specific disability, such as retardation, may find denial more difficult and acceptance more inevitable than a parent whose child's growth seemed to proceed normally for the first two years and whose disability may fall into the relatively less distinct categories of autism or minimal brain disfunction. The personality of the parents can also contribute substantially to their reaction. Psychologists sometimes refer to this as the *premorbid* personality, in that it reflects how the person was before the sudden onset of a particular emotional difficulty. Clearly some parents adjust better to the situation in terms of acceptance, while others continue to protest on behalf of themselves and their children or never overcome their huge sense of guilt and depression or the lack of it.

Support from family and friends is another significant factor in determining the nature of parents' reaction to a child's disability. Well-meaning grandparents may contribute to denial; insensitivities of relatives and friends may contribute to feelings of guilt or possible resentment on the part of parents. On the other hand, family and friends who are noncritical, open, and supportive influence the process of adjustment to the child's disability favorably.

Finally, I should mention the reaction of other children in the family to parents' ability to accept their child's disability. I have observed that more frequently than not other children lessen the impact through their more "innocent" reactions, questions, and concerns. There are feelings of guilt generated for parents attempting to avoid concentrating too much attention on the more needy disabled child, but the benefits for parents and children seem to outweigh the negative contributions of other siblings. This does not prevent many parents of developmentally disabled children from hesitating to have other children, even when this is the only child in the family. Undoubtedly, the guilt and even anger associated with the birth of the disabled child interferes with the risk of giving birth to and raising a second child.

RUNNING THE PROFESSIONAL GAUNTLET

As was noted before, pediatricians exhibit a general tendency to "reassure" parents by suggesting that they wait for development to take place before they take any action. This "wait and see, he'll outgrow it" attitude may cause the loss of valuable time for intervention and interfere with parents' psychological acceptance. An insistence by parents that there seems to be a delay in development is too frequently treated as a general overanxious reaction.

In the case of neurological degeneration, the loss of time can be critical. In some cases, the delay is justified, but too often it represents a lack of diagnostic competence on the part of the pediatrician and/or a personal anxiety on the part of the professional about the developmentally disabled. It is tempting to reassure parents and to spare them the anxiety associated with the search for a diagnosis, but very often it is a necessary crisis that must be faced.

A sensitive professional can be of great help in the process of dealing with a problem of developmental disability, even though the nature of the disability may not be clear. Parents are sometimes accused of "shopping around." Very often their search is justified, in that they have not found a professional advocate for their child. They may detect a professional bias in favor of a particular specialty or realize, as many parents do, that a judgment has been made on very little information.

It is true that the period of denial lends itself to searching for professional confirmation that nothing is wrong, but this soon leads to a more genuine concern for an accurate diagnosis. Unfortunately, the nature of many forms of developmental disability is such that they be multidetermined or that their etiology is ambiguous. How important is the diagnosis? I would respond by saying only if it contributes to the effectiveness of the treatment. The specialty bias continues to be a problem, in that each professional tends to view the child from his/her own frame of reference. Too few see the whole child, and, as a result, many developmentally disabled children carry a number of labels. What is essential to know are the major strengths and weaknesses of the child and how these may play a role in a growth-promoting, therapeutic, educative program designed for that individual. It is not that these children do not have disabilities in common or that the remediation techniques might not apply equally well in a variety of cases, but it is that the application of these techniques must be individually adapted to the best advantage of each child.

TWO MAJOR TASKS FOR PARENTS

In my experience, parents of developmentally disabled children must ultimately deal with two major tasks. The first task is finding an appropriate educative program for young children with developmental disabilities. Very often school districts caught in budgetary crises or unaware of the role they might play for young children have not developed adequate programs. Independent facilities must be developed and funded that place a great emphasis on parental involvement.

The second task involves letting go of the child, literally and figuratively. Guilt and other related feelings tend toward an especially over protective attitude, a feeling that no one else can take care of my child as I do. This, of course, may interfere with the potential growth of the child.

Parents whose children are finally involved in specially designed early school programs are often amazed by the capacities toward independence exhibited by their children. At first they may have some difficulty expressing their feelings, but they are very relieved that someone else appreciates the individuality of their disabled child and recognizes his or her competencies and can help to develop them.

PARENTS AS PARTNERS WITH PROFESSIONALS

This was the theme of a special issue of the professional journal *Exceptional Children.*[2] In that publication, several parents shared first-hand experiences of having developmentally disabled or otherwise handicapped children. Clearly, one helpful experience for parents is to share their experiences and their feelings about having a developmentally disabled child. Our finding in the parent groups at Little Village School is that this sharing is a significant part of the value of group meetings.

Kathryn Gorham, the Director of the Montgomery County Association for Retarded Citizens, Family and Community Services, in Silver Springs, Maryland, writes in the issue of *Exceptional Children* referred to above that parents and professionals must accept the fact that they are their disabled child's best advocate. As such, parents should make every effort to learn about their child's disabilities and available community resources. A passive attitude, waiting to be told what to do, is not in the best interest of either parent or child. Making suggestions and asking questions are not to be thought of as "being nosy." Gorham feels, in fact, that parents should retain the records of their children rather than wait helplessly while their reports may or may not get sent from one agency to another after the necessary releases have been signed. This facilitates communication between professionals, and keeps parents informed of their child's status. Well-informed parents can help to integrate the material collected from all sources, including the detailed observations of their child at home.

Parents need to develop their observation skills. Detailed home observations are extremely useful for purposes of diagnosis and monitoring the effects of medication. They also help the behavioral psychologist suggest alternative ways of dealing with difficult parent-child interactions, such as toilet training or controlling unwanted behavior, e.g. destructiveness. Gorham suggests that parents should also keep accurate written records of visits to doctors, questions asked and the answers. I would emphasize the importance of parental records of developmental milestones and of the onset, duration, and termination of treatment modalities. By sharing information with each other and with professionals, the parents of a developmentally disabled child will not only help themselves and their own child, but all children who suffer from similar handicaps.

The identification and, where necessary, the creation of community resources for developmentally disabled children is another effort parents undertake. Parents who detect a need for a particular service for their child can assume that the need exists for others as well. Special classes and schools, recreation opportunities, specially trained dentists and pediatricians all fall within this category. The sharing of these resources and identifying common needs is another important function of our parent groups at Little Village.

SOME GUIDELINES FOR PROFESSIONALS

There is no doubt that the service to developmentally disabled children and their families has been significantly improved in recent years. While the various disciplines of pediatrics, obstetrics, neurology, psychology, social work, and speech and special education have made great strides, there is still a good deal more that can be done given our present state of knowledge, particularly by individual practitioners. I would offer the following guidelines to any professional working with the developmentally disabled child:

1. Be aware of the "whole" child, including the family.

2. Try to avoid looking at the child from the vantage point of your own area of specialization exclusively.

3. Be aware of the parents of the developmentally disabled child's sensitivities concerning such matters as the child's future, diagnostic labels, and the source of the child's disabilities.

4. Try to avoid presenting either a hopeless attitude or a "Pollyannaish" one. Offer hope whenever possible, but be realistic.

5. Be aware of the parents of the developmentally disabled child's tendencies to project blame and/or feel guilty and about their possible feelings of impotence. These are "real" feelings even though they are not always objectively based.

6. Learn how to help the parents accept their child's disability. If you follow the suggestions offered above and avoid being critical or offhand with parents, their acceptance of the problems to be encountered by their children and themselves is heightened. It is the only way to responsibly discharge your professional responsibility, no matter what your expertise.

7. Learn about community resources. The total care of the developmentally disabled child involves many facets of his or her existence. A single approach, whether it be psychotherapeutic, biochemical, or educational, is not likely to be effective. You can assure a greater success for your efforts and spare the child and parents a great deal of wasted, unhappy time if you are knowledgeable about what services are available and have some specific information to offer.

8. Finally, allow parents to contribute meaningfully in the process of helping their disabled children. As I indicated above, these parents have energy and knowledge to offer and, after all, have a greater stake in the rehabilitation process for their child than the professional.

The largest strides in overcoming disabilities has come about when parents have joined individually and in organizations to publicize, lobby, raise funds, and to generally create conditions where professionals are inspired to do more than maintain a status quo in care. Parent groups have been able to tip the balance in favor of research and development of new techniques for identification and treatment of developmental disabilities. Early identification of disabilities is now a national priority, because of the combined efforts of professionals and parents. This "partnership" is even more critical now as we begin to develop the programs to meet these needs.

REFERENCES

1. Frank, J.D.: Individual differences in certain aspects of the level of aspiration. *Am J Psychol, 47*:119-128, 1935.
2. Gorham, K.A.: A lost generation of parents. *Except Child, 41, 8*:521-525, 1975.
3. Kanner, L.: Early infantile autism. *J Pediatr, 25*:211-217, 1944.
4. Kübler-Ross, E.: *On Death and Dying.* New York, MacMillan, 1969.

CHAPTER 11.

A TOTAL MILIEU APPROACH TO HANDICAPPED INFANT EDUCATION

CLAIRE SALANT, M.A.

"You're an overanxious mother. Your baby will out grow it."

"Nothing can be done until your baby begins to walk, then we'll see."

"Don't take this baby home. It's a vegetable. Put it in an institution."

"Nobody knows what it's like. I don't go out of the house anymore. I'm the only one he'll eat for."

"I know there's something wrong with my baby but nobody will pay attention."

These statements and scores like these were the reasons for the development of the TMA (Total Milieu Approach) Infant Program at the Suffolk Rehabilitation Center, Commack, Long Island, New York. Located in Western Suffolk County, the center offers comprehensive, medical, therapeutic, and emotional and diagnostic services and treatment to handicapped children and their families in Suffolk County.

Funded as a demonstration project through the Handicapped Children's Early Education Program, Bureau of Education for the Handicapped, United States Office of Education, Washington, D.C., a model infant program evolved over a three-year period.

Over 150 babies have been a part of this program, ranging from four days old to thirty months. They represent the widest possible spectrum of physical and mental handicapping condition. Some babies have been high risk because of the birth or family history, such as the son of a fifteen-year-old mother, the new baby in a family where four older siblings have specific learning disabilities. Some babies are born profoundly physically or mentally disabled. Still others have rare genetic-based myopathies. Twelve of the babies died before they reached their second birthday.

PROGRAM OVERVIEW

The TMA Project was designed to enhance the infants' natural environment, establishing a total milieu to assist in preventing and modifying some of the physical, sensorimotor, perceptual, and emotional impediments to optimum adjustment, learning, and performance.

The curriculum design is an innovative approach concentrating on careful preparation and commitment of the prime caregiver (parent) and the professional team together to provide richness of experiences not usually available to the handicapped infant. The professional team is composed of an audiologist, infant teacher, physical rehabilitation therapist, physician, psychologist, social worker, speech pathologist, and consultant medical services, as needed.   An optimal learning environment is developed, facilitating each infant's physical, social, emotional, cognitive, and language development and communication skills. For the infant, the educational model is the home, rather than the school, with his/her mother, or prime caregiver, being the most crucial person in that model. The uniqueness of each infant and family is respected, realistically taking into account each specific home and family as it exists, utilizing that which is culturally significant to the infant and his/her family. The infant teacher makes regular visits to the home to work with the infant and the caregiver. While an average visit is approximately two hours weekly, the infant teacher may find it necessary to visit daily for a period, if a family is in distress. Each mother, or prime caregiver, in the TMA Infant Program, participates in both general and specific activities planned to increase her awareness and involvement in the program as well as her acceptance of the handicapped baby. Sessions on child development relating to all aspects of infancy and early childhood are conducted by the infant team. Individual and group counseling for families and extended families, feeding, and other appropriate therapies, are provided in the Center and at home, with great flexibility in response to the individual needs of each family. Beginning with the initial contact, the parents' participation and feedback is an integral part of the total process of program developed.

INFANT CURRICULUM

The "sacred cows" of the preschool curriculum—circle, square, and triangle—have to be replaced by the bottle and the rattle. Far more basic than learning colors, is learning about your body and yourself. Changing diapers, feeding, and bathing may well be the baby's most important educational functions. Clothed in language, these earliest experiences are the baby's first discovery of the world. In the responses she receives to his or her own cries for food, for attention, for care, she/he learns to trust and to respond to the environment and the people in it.

The handicapped baby coming into the world with sensory and/or motor impairments may find his experiences distorted, limited, or incomprehensible. He may tune out people, lose his motivation, and become passive or an unsatisfied and constantly demanding baby. The normal areas of mouthing, reaching, and grabbing may be available only limitedly to this baby or not at all with his brain unable to control his body's movements.

Through the normal life experiences, each baby is given the chance to have to explore, to touch, to reach through adaptions of materials, environment, and personal handling. In the atmosphere of the baby's home, the infant teacher can assist each caregiver and each family to understand the baby's functioning so that all handling becomes therapeutic and enriching.

Each baby is assessed to determine his development level, deficits, strengths, and interests as the basis of curriculum building. Appropriate toys are left in each home, either brought by the infant teacher or made by the family for all to enjoy. Each baby's curriculum is individually designed, because each baby is different as is the ability of the caregiver at any point in time.

The infant teacher, in the home, carries through all of the suggestions and recommendations of the team. For example, if the baby is on a feeding program to increase oral normalization, the teacher would begin to visit at lunch time. Her presence is encouraging to a mother whose baby might be gagging at unfamiliar foods. She would bring food to taste with different textures and shapes, making sure the baby is seated properly, naming the foods and interacting socially, and most important of all, keeping mealtime a pleasant family experience.

It is only by going to the child's home that one knows the realities of what is or is not possible. Certainly a one-room apartment cannot hold extensive adaptive equipment; a mother with other children cannot ignore their needs.

In the intimacy of the home, parent and teacher develop great trust and respect.

THE ASSESSMENT PROCESS

The assessments, too, are made by the interdisciplinary team in order to truly understand the functioning of each baby. Infant teachers are responsible for approximately eight families and accompany them to all initial and follow up assessments. The teachers also may provide transportation, baby-sit for siblings so both parents can come to the Center, and act as the family's advocate. Some assessments may be done at home, if the baby is most comfortable and a truer perception of the baby's functioning is then possible.

A parent-attitude form is filled out by the parents before service begins and then yearly. A Center-developed Motor Rating Scale, Receptive and Expressive Language Scale, and Feeding Evaluation are administered to each baby. Completing the assessment are a medical and social work evaluation and the Bayley Scales of Infant Development. Alternate test equipment has been designed for the Bayley Scales, which were standardized on normal infants with toys and tasks difficult for the handicapped baby to handle. The parents, teachers, and therapists may also participate in the testing, so that the baby is in the best possible position to perform to his capacity. It is an attempt to circumvent the deleterious effect of physical and sensory handicaps on a mental test score. The purpose is to more clearly understand each child's functioning without violating the integrity of a standardized instrument. Bayley Scale reevaluations occur at six-month milestones so that a rate of growth can be understood, a far more significant factor than an isolated score.

STAFF DEVELOPMENT

Staff involved with infant programs require unique skills and training. All training is done with the entire team, so that all team members develop a common language and philosophy. It is not sufficient to be a talented infant educator or therapist—one must also be an adult educator, since the quality of the program depends upon the ability of the staff to teach the parents how to handle their baby.

Each team member must be able to work on a team, contributing to other members and learning from them in turn. Each team member must learn about the different disciplines and be able to share the knowledge and skill of her own. Above all, each member must be open and sharing, knowing when they disagree and expressing their views.

Each team member is a mental health worker who must be given skills to deal with families in a crisis. The infant teacher sitting at the table over a cup of coffee with the mother may be the one the mother trusts most to share her pain. She cannot then refuse to listen and run for the social worker. It is our obligation to provide her with the skills she will need to fulfill her function optimally. Not only do families have crises — so does the staff. The quickest way to "burn staff out" is to leave staff members isolated in the field without adequate skills and support.

Infant teachers in the TMA program spend a month in the Center learning about the other therapeutic fields and practicing with babies in therapy. They then get apprenticed to an experienced teacher to observe home visits before they are assigned their own case-load of eight families. Every eighth week is spent back at the Center sharing information and seeing babies together.

Weekly team meetings review individual baby's programs in depth so that they stay relevant and consistent.

Formal in-service training has included courses on the following:

1. Neurodevelopment approach to physical rehabilitation
2. Understanding Piaget
3. Normal motor development (birth — three years)
4. Feeding technique
5. Normal development of play (birth — three years)
6. Dealing with death
7. Family and staff crisis
8. Mental health technique for nonmental health professionals

CONCLUSION

There are a variety of models of infant programs existing today — the TMA is just one of those models. It has been effective: It has provided much needed service at a crucial time in a family's life, becoming a vehicle for public education and the alerting of parents and professionals alike.

Infant education is still a new field. Few training programs of any kind explore the first three years of life or prepare professionals to work with babies. There are even fewer parent-education programs and certainly none that anticipate the birth of a handicapped baby. The truth is that everyone wants a lovely, healthy baby, and the birth of a handicapped baby is an experience combining shock, disbelief, and overwhelming distress. It cuts across socioeconomic, ethnic, or racial lines. It has been described as similar to the process one undergoes when a loved one dies, because there is indeed a period of mourning for the death of the "normal" child. Professionals must respect the stage of reconciliation of the parents without judgment. While no one can take away the pain, we can stand alongside and share, be supportive, and work with the families.

Some babies will overcome their handicaps and go into the mainstream. For others, the damage is too severe for any future beyond a very sheltered one. Early intervention gives each baby the chance to develop to his potential and leaves no family with the devastation of "if only . . . ."

Example of Infant Curriculum

SUFFOLK REHABILITATION CENTER FOR THE PHYSICALLY HANDICAPPED, INC.

NAME	DATE OF BIRTH	UNIT NO.
Ellen		

Home Teaching Activities

Language

To help facilitate language comprehension, encourage parents to provide constant, speaking stimulation to help build Ellen's identification and listening vocabulary. Recognize opportune moments to teach through daily contacts (dressing, feeding, bathing, and playing, etc.). Avoid confusing Ellen (by using short sentences and simple vocabulary). Use the word "shoes" when her shoes are being put on; "fingers" when her fingers are touched, etc.

Use simple sentences, songs and finger plays. Familiarize her with action words:

Go get your shoes
Pick up your spoon
Clap your hands
Let's run, etc.

Avoid using two or more words to denote the same thing so as to avoid confusion *cat;* not cat, kitten, *and* kitty, etc.

Repeat the names of people, objects, and actions that are familiar to Ellen, in the hope of building her vocabulary comprehension.

Reinforce any jabbering, babbling, etc., by responding with words and praise in the effort to encourage her to use her voice more often as a means of communication and as a method for getting what she wants.

Instead of having Ellen's clothes and toys right at hand, leave some of her things in another room. Encourage a response to "Go get your doll. It is by the bed," etc.

Body Image

Simple songs, games, and finger plays encourage self-awareness.

"Put your finger in the air"
"Where, oh where is Ellen?"
"Open them, shut them"
"Come on and sing with me"
"Hokey, Pokey" (eliminate left and right)

Doll Activities

Dressing and undressing
Bathing
Singing
Identifying body parts, combing hair, etc.

Mirror Activities

Hold Ellen in front of large mirror, sing and do motions to body image songs, move out of mirror ask "Where's Ellen?" Move back in — touch Ellen. Point to her in the mirror and say "Where's Ellen?" Do the same with Mommy, Daddy, and Anthony. Touch and name body parts in the mirror. Undress Ellen in front of large mirror, say "Where are your shoes?" Take them off, say "We took off your shoes!" Hold them in front of the mirror and say, "We see the shoes." Repeat with other articles of clothing.

Books

Use homemade books and pictures of familiar people and objects. As she is shown the pictures, incorporate the following:

"Look at the baby's eyes."
Touch her eyes and say, "Here are your eyes."
Then ask, "Where are your eyes?"

Do this for parts of body, clothing, household items, and family members, etc.

Auditory Stimulation

When there is activity in various rooms of the house (preparing dinner, washing machine running, telephone ringing, etc.):

take Ellen where she can hear the sound — explain the sounds to her:

The telephone is ringing
Listen to the washing machine, etc.
Do the same outdoors:
Listen to the car
I hear the dog barking
Encourage her to produce sounds:
Bang drum
Knock down blocks
Shake rattles (etc.)

Tactile

1. Sand and water play with appropriate props.
2. Place various objects in her hand to let her touch and feel the difference between them.
3. Touch different parts of her body with various textures: a feather, penny, wool, etc.
4. Provide her with opportunities to feel the textures of different surfaces such as grass, sand, and wood.
5. Use tickling, jumping, physical action games, hugging, etc. to express pleasure in her accomplishments.

Fine Motor

1. Spontaneous scribbling on paper
2. Simple circle puzzle
3. Put pennies in bank, or buttons in can
4. Stringing large beads
5. Pull-apart toys (pop beads)
6. Stacking toys
7. Wrap yarn on her hands or feet — let her remove it

Gross Motor

1. Use pull and push toys
2. Jumping and crawling activities
3. Rolling on grass
4. Walking up steps

5. Swinging
6. Riding toys
7. Ring-around-a-rosy
8. Climbing in and out of boxes, etc.

Problem-solving Activities

1. Simple — one– or two-piece puzzles.
2. Drop plastic spoons, pennies, etc. into a container; demonstrate how to remove them.
3. Encourage Ellen to imitate.
4. Hide a piece of candy, raisin, etc. under a cup. Be certain she observes the action. Encourage her to find the hidden object.
5. Hide and seek — hide behind a chair or door; say "Where's Mommy?" Encourage her to find mother. Do the same with toys (leave part of toy showing a little bit) .

It will be important to observe Ellen carefully and take advantage of the times she is interested and wants to participate in a learning activity. Also, be observant to note when she has passed the point when the activity is productive. Take advantage of her high interest levels in music and motion to build language comprehension and cognitive skills. Be ready to shift to another learning activity or to postpone the activity when her interest is low. This will be especially important to remember when encouraging her in problem-solving games.

Choose activities and toys that will give Ellen immediate success and reinforce her with praise in the form of clapping, smiling, hugging, cheering (to which she responds with pleasure) , etc.

CHAPTER 12.

BIOFEEDBACK WITH YOUNG CEREBRAL PALSIED CHILDREN

LEONARD SILVERSTEIN, Ph.D.

THE DEVELOPMENT of precise, specific motor control has been established elsewhere.[1] The enhancement of learning control of unconscious motor processes has only been limited by the provision of appropriate feedback. The capacity of the nervous system to control voluntary motor activity by use of a sequence of auditory clicks is quite extensive. Biofeedback with the cerebral palsied, however, presents unique theoretical and methodological problems. This report is an attempt to deal with some of these issues and provide a road map for others who are interested in working with the developmentally disabled.

One theoretical issue concerns the plasticity of the brain and its ability to develop new pathways where previous damage precludes normal feedback cues. Because of the nature of cerebral palsy, the children enrolled in the Nassau County Cerebral Palsy Center have either damaged output or input sensorimotor channels or both. Special provisions are necessary to present information via the most "intact" sensory channel and providing rewards for responding with the correct motor output. In a manner of speaking, our emphasis was on "accentuating the positive and eliminating the negative." The literature on controlling physiological responses indicates that the techniques are referred to as *voluntary control procedures* or as *operant conditioning*. For our purposes, a voluntary response was defined as one that is reliably influenced by an instructional stimulus. As operant was defined as a response that was under the control of a discriminative stimulus. The paradigms can be illustrated diagramatically as follows:

Operant Model

S discriminitive   : R operant   S reinforcing

Voluntary Model

S instructional   : R voluntary   S feedback

In spite of the similarity of these paradigms, the theoretical structure associated with operant and feedback approaches to learned motor control differ in a significant way. The development of instructional control depends on verbal labels (keep your "head up") with internal cues (striate muscle contraction) of the act. In addition, the pairing of the verbal stimuli with a device that buzzes or lights up as a consequence of keeping your "head up" was used. What has evolved is a form of higher-order operant conditioning. The original intent was to mechanize the reinforcing stimuli through an extensive bioengineering effort. This was conceptualized as a form of environmental enrichment. The environment was altered to provide reinforcement by a device that would never tire or become emotionally upset due to the failure of the child to respond. In fact, what evolved was an intensive effort to use higher-order conditioning to get the behavior going. The programs to be described were the result of verbal cues and other forms of attention seeking, which were used to get the child to "tune in" to the relevant stimuli. These cues were selected by observation and discussion with parents, therapists, teachers, and others involved with the care of the cerebral palsy child.

One female five-years, five-months old, with mixed generalized tension athetosis and spasticity of a severe degree was observed to sit up in class 9.8 percent of the time. She earned a social quotient (Vineland Social Maturity Scale) of five months. Her intellectual development as measured by the Full Range Picture Vocabulary test was two years, six months. The team of psychologist, therapists, and teachers set a goal of having her "sit up" so that she could benefit from instruction. A chair was constructed that was shaped as a channel, and a pulley system was attached which played music (reinforcing event) whenever she sat up. Within sixteen sessions of a one–half hour each she was sitting up 72.04 percent of the time. In two independent reversals, she averaged 46.9 percent total time sitting up. A follow-up four months later revealed that the child was sitting up 71.29 percent of the time (nonreinforced).

However, the child was observed to be using abnormal hyper-extensive patterns to achieve this behavior. In order to reduce those patterns and to prompt her to hold her head erect without abnormal reflex patterns, a series of switching devices was attached to her chair (Fig. 12–1). Upon touching these switches, the child received auditory feedback (tone) about her head position. The music was played when her head was within a twenty-degree vertical cone. Higher-order conditioning in the form of verbal cues was discontinued. She now sits up approximately 50 percent of the time without abnormal hyperextension. Training will continue until her behavior plateaus.

The general conclusion is that it is possible to reduce abnormal movement with the appropriate combination of rewards (music) and feedback cues (verbal, tone, etc.). The use of devices

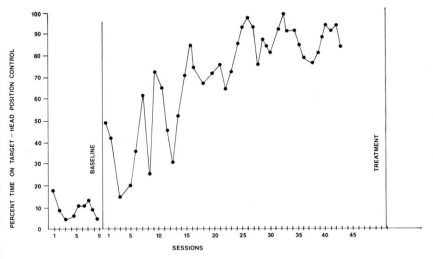

Figure 12-1. Head position control for the reduction of abnormal hyper-extension.

has not obviated the need for trained therapeutic personnel. Rather, in the hands of the dedicated professional, it provides another useful tool in overcoming the handicaps of the developmentally disabled.

Progress in Reducing Athetoid Movements
Subject: M.P.

A five-year-old male was diagnosed as a severe athetoid cerebral palsy. He could not raise his hand in the classroom without engaging in a great deal of extraneous muscle activity. The strategy for obtaining movement was to tense his muscles the entire day. M.P.'s first target behavior was to achieve greater body stability as measured by a stabilometer, a device that measures total body activity. The stabilometer was placed under a straight-backed, slope-seat chair, fitted with a lapboard.

The effect of the stabilometer was to magnify the movement of M.P. and thereby provide sensory feedback via the tilting chair. No other form of information was provided, and in the period from February 2, 1975 to June 24, 1975, an increased level of stability was noted (from 15% to 80% time of target). Since M.P. was able to decrease his extra movements without apparent feedback, a light mounted to his laptray was provided as positive feedback. The stabilometer setting was made more sensitive and the magnitude of the task was increased by requiring greater head stability. Head stability was measured by a mercury switch attached to a cloth strap helmet that measured angular deviation from the upright. This concurrent paradigm, head stability and overall body movement, was induced with the instruction, "Keep the light on." Using this concurrent task (Fig. 12-2A and B), a baseline level of 2.17 percent was obtained for time on target. The presence of the light on the laptray facilitated integration within the classroom. The combined task behavior was emitted at a 16.25 percent total time on target. No type of reinforcement, other than verbal praise, had been used. The plan was to continue the feedback all through the day until the behavior levels off and then, and perhaps, select other goals.

The main thrust of this program involved gross motor move-

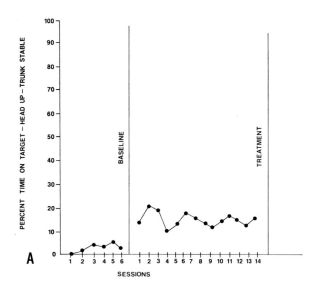

Figure 12-2A and 12-2B.   Time on target for child M.P. in concurrent paradigm for head control and trunk stability.

ments of the athetoid cerebral palsy child. Corrective action began when the excessive movements were translated into a moving/tilting chair phenomenon. From a theoretical viewpoint, overcorrection provided a supply of response images that are possibly left in memory by experience. This involuntary performance may be the first prerequisite of voluntary movements. The use of a feedback light enables the child to increase the ability to pair external stimuli with internal consequences of muscle tightening. Pairing of the verbal labels, "turn the light on" with "sitting still with head up" help the individual to identify and calibrate. The consistent covariation lead to improved performance. Further improvement remains an empirical question, to be programmed by bioengineering of more effective knowledge of results. The photograph 12-2B depicts two children racing slot cars by maintaining correct head position. Verbal encouragement by teachers and peers represents a higher order of incentive that may prove a useful tool in the biofeedback training of cerebral palsied children. This approach will be the basis of a future report.

REFERENCE

1. Basmajian, J.U.: *Muscles Alive: Their Functions Revealed by Electromyography.* Williams & Wilkins, 1962.

CHAPTER 13.

LANGUAGE-DISORDERED CHILDREN:
A Neuropsychologic View*†

BARBARA C. WILSON, Ph.D.
JAMES J. WILSON, Ph.D.

WE SHOULD like to discuss some of the etiologies of atypical language development, the related problems of differential diagnosis and assessment, and finally, a method of presenting assessment data that appears useful in arriving at intervention strategies.

First, some definitions: *Language* is here defined as a socially derived, transmissible system of symbols used for communication, which need not be verbal. Rules, called *grammar,* govern its usage. Language is thought to be necessary for most cognitive endeavors,[27] is the stuff of which "thought" is made, and appears to be the most efficient mode of communication of thought.[29,33] Our neuropsychologic bias suggests that delayed or deviant language development is always a result of central nervous system dysfunction, and only in extreme instances of social or emotional deprivation is delayed language environmentally determined.

Inadequate language development is thought to impede acquisition of academic skills.[6] The limitations imposed by inadequate communication have their effects on social and emotional development as well. It is only in the past fifteen to twenty years that

*The work reported here was supported in part by Grant 0-74-0545 from the Bureau of Education for the Handicapped, Office of Education, Department of Health, Education and Welfare.
†This paper is based in part on a paper presented to the Conference on Developmental Disorders in Early Childhood, sponsored by Little Village School, Merrick, New York, and Sagamore Children's Center, Melville, New York, and held at Melville, New York, April, 1977.

developmental language disorders have been recognized as a diagnostic entity and that the processes underlying language acquisition have been subject to systematic study. Although speech therapy for children has been with us for a long time, the language pathologist concerned with children's language rather than with post stroke adult aphasia is a fairly recent phenomenon. The literature explosion in the area of developmental language disorders is evidence of increased interest and concern and continues to highlight how little we know.

ETIOLOGY

What *do* we know about the etiologies of developmental language disorders? Precious little, and much of it inferential, at best. The relatively large numbers of children who present with deficits in language development and who are products of high risk pregnancies or births or who had stormy neonatal courses suggest that organic factors probably play a role. We are talking about children in whom no "hard signs" of neurologic impairment can be detected.

In a study of twenty-two language-disordered children, seven to twelve years of age, neurologic examination found six to have "hard signs" and twelve to have high-risk histories.[35] In our ongoing study of children in the Preschool Development Program,‡ approximately 50 percent are considered to have probable organic deficits in the absence of a positive neurologic examination but with high risk birth or neonatal histories. The children who have such histories cannot be detected from among others on the basis of common cognitive, linguistic, perceptual, or motor deficits; that is, they do not demonstrate a constellation of deficits that constitutes a syndrome.

Other frequent observations concerning children with com-

‡The Preschool Development Program provides service to two-and-one-half– to five-year-old children with primary language disorders. It received its first three years of funding as a demonstration project from the Bureau of Education for the Handicapped, Office of Education, Department of Health, Education and Welfare. It is currently funded by the New York State Education Department, the Roslyn Chapter of the National Council of Jewish Women, the Roslyn Presbyterian Church, and the North Shore University Hospital.

munication disorders are the relatively high number of affected sibs, a history of delayed speech or language development in the family, and reports of reading disability in the family. All of this is suggestive of a genetic factor, one similar, perhaps, to that underlying Critchley's "developmental dyslexia."[15] In our experience, children with such family histories do not demonstrate distinctive patterns of function and dysfunction. They, too, fail to demonstrate a "syndrome."

Hearing impairment and mental retardation are two major causes of delayed acquisition of speech and language and clearly differ in etiology from the less-well-defined communication disorders. Both are worth mentioning here nonetheless, since we know that one of the most frequently overlooked diagnoses in young children with delayed language is hearing impairment,[34] while the language delay seen in retarded children typically differs from that of the child with deviant language development.[5,6]

A hearing impairment is more difficult to detect than deafness, particularly in the very young child. A child may have sufficient hearing to understand and to learn some language — just enough for him to appear emotionally disturbed or mentally retarded. These are not uncommon diagnoses for children with undetected hearing losses. The impact on their cognitive and linguistic development is, in many areas, palpable.[40] We know that any hearing loss is potentially detrimental to overall development, and frequently information obtained in a detailed history will be suggestive of such a problem. A history of sensorineural deafness in other family members suggests a genetic factor; a history of frequent ear infection suggests the possibility of a conductive loss. Kernicterus secondary to neonatal hyperbilirubinemia can result in any or all of the aspects of the "unholy trinity": athetosis (cerebral palsy), vertical gaze palsy, and a high-frequency hearing loss. In any case, a child who presents with a delay in language development, regardless of history, should have a complete audiological evaluation, repeated until a reliable estimate is obtained.

Language levels among retarded children are typically consonant with their overall cognitive development and hence, in relation to population norms, are delayed in language acquisition. However, the literature suggests that acquisition of most of the syntactic and phonologic rules occurs by the age of four in normally developing children.[8,29] There is further indication that the language of retarded children with an M.A. of 4 or more develops in normal sequence[26] and can be expected to continue to develop into early adolescence.[27] There are some mentally retarded children whose language skills are more deficient than their M.A.'s would suggest. These children may have "measles and a broken leg" — two (probably) unrelated disabilities; retardation and a developmental language disorder.

Autistic children are yet another group that demonstrates significant delay in acquisition of communication skills. Autism has moved from a descriptor to a diagnosis, and by implication, to a prognosis[17] or, as Ritvo puts it, "from adjective to noun."[36] Although there have long been differences in theoretical formulations among clinical investigators, autism has been viewed by many — and for a long time — as a primary emotional disorder.[3,25,28] The conclusions of Ritvo and others reflect those of an increasing number of investigators and clinicians who agree that autism is a "physical disease of the brain."[36] When an entire diagnostic group can be characterized by two salient features, deficient communication and an affective disturbance, one is hard pressed *not* to conclude that similar *physical* mechanisms underlie the syndrome. There are other characteristics which are frequently seen in the autistic child, but not in obligatory association.[10-14]

For those of us with a neuropsychologic orientation, the systematic nature of the primary disabilities exhibited by the autistic child — affective and communicative — leads to a consideration of the ascending reticular activating system and the limbic and temporal lobes of the brain as probable areas of dysfunction. Two recent papers have provided the first hard evidence of such brain-behavior relationships. Dalby*[16] studied 327 children with a diagnosis of language disorder. Of these, 65 percent showed signs of brain damage. Pneumoencephalograms were

*This paper has not yet been published. It is available from M.A. Dalby, Neurological University Department, Aarhus University, Aarhus, Denmark.

obtained in 161 cases.   A significant number showed atrophic lesions of the left temporal lobe ("language area") as compared to children with petit mal and intact language.

Hauser et al.[22] studied seventeen children diagnosed as autistic. Pneumoencephalograms in fifteen out of seventeen demonstrated the presence of dilated left ventricles and structural abnormalities in the left temporal lobes. Such anatomic correlates come as no surprise if one relates the disordered behaviors to probable loci of damage within the brain. The mesial temporal structures are part of the limbic system, which is crucial to the mediation of drives and emotion and is also involved in learning. The lateral temporal lobes are concerned with the processing of auditory information. The left temporal lobe is thought to be the primary processor of linguistic input. These behavioral-neurologic correlates are admittedly an oversimplification in attempting to define the substrates of a syndrome as complex as autism. They do seem to lead one in a hypothesis–testing direction, however, and suggest a hypothetical set of language development continua — from intact to delayed to deviant to something more global in its impact, i.e. autism. It is these hypothetically related continua that provide a basis for considering the Dalby and Hauser data together.

The schematic diagram in Figure 13-1 suggests that measurable language development in terms of syntax, semantics and

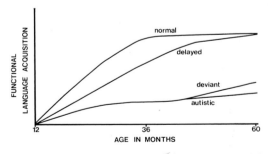

Figure 13-1. Hypothetical continua suggesting the relationships among rates of functional language acquisition in linguistically normal, delayed, deviant, and autistic children.

phonology starts at twelve months. With the exception of semantics, which continues to develop over a longer period of time, language development in the normally developing child is virtually complete by four years.[27] The child with delayed language development gets to the same place, but more slowly. The child with deviant language development, whose language is not unfolding in normal sequence, usually reaches a plateau of linguistic competence at a lower level than the normal or delayed group. Somewhere along this last continuum stands the *swing child,* who has been, is, and will be called *severely language disordered, language disordered with autistic features* or simply *autistic,* depending on the professional bias of the evaluator.

There is yet another group, and perhaps the largest, comprised of children with developmental language disorders who are neither hearing impaired, neurologically impaired by examination or history, whose family histories do not suggest a genetic etiology, nor are they autistic or retarded. Their deficits, too, reflect atypical central nervous system activity. We may conceptualize their deficits as referable to differences in their neurochemistry, to temporal variations at the synapses, to differences in neural circuits — to any hypothetical construct relating brain function to linguistic behavior. We need not assume, however, that these children are brain damaged in the classic sense. In the absence of neurologic findings, relevant history or a high-risk pregnancy, the rule of parsimony should apply.

In summary, we do not know a great deal about the etiologies of language deficits. We know that hearing impaired children are frequently inadequately evaluated; we know that genetic factors appear to underlie some instances of the disability; we know that high-risk pregnancies and deliveries are over-represented, and it is our position that all language disorders in children reflect central nervous system dysfunction except in instances of extreme deprivation. We know that many children with primary language disorders continue to be seen as primarily retarded, autistic, "brain damaged," schizophrenic, emotionally disturbed . . . We know we have problems in differential diagnosis.

DIFFERENTIAL DIAGNOSIS

At the point of initial evaluation, how can we make a distinction between the language-delayed and language-disordered child and between these and the retarded or autistic child? Frequently we cannot, and only ongoing diagnostic evaluations and preferably diagnostically oriented teaching, will help.

There are some guidelines, however. We start from the position that speech and language development, like motor development, is guided by maturational processes. Clinical experience and the literature suggest that developmental delays or abberations rarely occur in isolation.[23,24,39] In attempting to make a differential diagnosis, more than speech and language must be sampled. The test profile of the retarded child, for example, tends to be flat across functional areas. Scores obtained on measures of linguistic, cognitive, and perceptual skills tend to be uniformly depressed, with the occasional exception of a "splinter skill." As Berry points out, "all dimensions of coding language — sensory-motor input, integration, retention, formulation, and expression — are uniformly affected."[5] A child whose test performance is equally depressed when instructions are given verbally and nonverbally, when stimuli are auditory, visual, perhaps tactile and kinesthetic as well, in whom no systematic pattern of higher function can be demonstrated in one modality over another, and in whom the synchrony between motor and language milestones is typically preserved may be considered mentally retarded. Qualifications include significant brain damage, emotional disorders, and hearing loss. This is in contrast to the child who appears to be functioning at a retarded level when asked to deal with auditory-linguistic stimuli, and/or when the desired response is oral-expressive. Using more appropriate, less verbal test instruments, tapping other than aural-oral channels, evaluating play and spontaneous gesture language will frequently make it clear that the child is not retarded, but has a language deficit. We assume that a hearing evaluation is routinely included as part of any of these evaluations.

The distinction between delayed language development and deviant language development is frequently difficult to make.

The distinctions are more than academic, since one would conceivably program differently in each instance. We can start with the general hypothesis that children with delayed language reflect a lag in the development of relevant neurologic systems, while deviant language development reflects pathologic neurological activity, neural structures, or damaged substrates. At one extreme is the child whose language output is phonologically, syntactically, and semantically appropriate, whose speech and language is following a normal developmental sequence, but whose rate of linguistic development is delayed. This, in contrast to the child whose developmental sequences are significantly disrupted, whose syntax is garbled, whose semantic usage may not convey meaning, whose receptive skills may be clearly deficient, and whose linguistic and motor milestones are typically out of synchrony.[27] Difficulties in differentiating the delayed from the deviant occur when the delay is moderate to severe and the deviance is mild to moderate. I do not believe we have the right questions, hence we have not developed the appropriate instruments needed to make these distinctions with good reliability.

The distinction between a developmental language disorder and autism can be thought of as a distinction in the degree of central nervous system derangement, and in the specific systems which are additionally disrupted in the autistic child. Areas other than language are typically found to be delayed in both the autistic and nonautistic child. However, the autistic child is much more disordered across many systems.[4,12,18,19,31,32] Although Churchill[9] has pointed out that among both developmentally language disordered and autistic children one sees abnormal responses to auditory stimuli, delay in acquisition of linguistic skills, and frequently, deficits in articulation, Griffith and Ritvo[21] indicate that when language-disordered children do learn to communicate verbally, they do not show the lack of "communicative intent and emotion" and delayed scholastic achievement characteristic of the autistic child. As Bartak, Rutter, and Cox[2] point out, the language disability of the verbal autistic child is both more severe and more deviant than that of children with developmental language disorders.

Distinctions must be made, too, among the various faces of language disorders. Just as we know that there is no single neurologic deficit which is necessary and sufficient to explain the range of language deficits one sees clinically, so, too, do we know that language disorders do not constitute a single syndrome. There are clusters or subsets of language disorders that must be capable of description in objective terms and will eventually be related to neural structures and processes. In our own work, we have been attempting to define these subsets along multiple dimensions and will touch upon this further in the following discussion of assessment and profiling.

Although secondary emotional disorders are doubtlessly involved, the difficulties encountered with expressive and/or receptive language experienced by language-disordered children must contribute massively to the picture of poor relatedness and unresponsiveness which they frequently present. In contrast to the autistic child, the child with a language disorder can relate by gestures, facial expressions, or "body talk." Such a child is receptive to and appears to comprehend the gestures and expressions of others. They can and do learn to make their needs known.[37]

As the workers in the field of autism come more and more to the position that autism is a neurologic rather than a psychiatric disorder, the nature of parental involvement will change, and so will our problem-solving strategies change. In the end, I believe that Rutter's question, "Autism — A central disorder of cognition and language?"[37] will be answered resoundingly in the affirmative.

ASSESSMENT AND PROFILE ANALYSIS

Now, to assessment: There are two opening points to be made, and several to dwell upon. First, no formal assessment defines the child. It is, rather, a first approximation, a basis for hypothesis testing and for the development of initial intervention strategies. A detailed history, systematic observation, and time are needed to flesh out the formal assessment.

Second, an assessment, albeit a first approximation, should provide useful information to those working with the child. So often an evaluation report is not helpful and is filed and forgotten. The bridge between evaluation data and intervention strategies — the translation from one discipline's frame of reference to another — is faulty, obscure, and most often, nonexistent. In the absence of more adequate interdisciplinary communication, the interveners, i.e. educators, and language pathologists, too frequently teach to a subtest score. "Johnny has low Auditory Association and Grammatic Closure scores on the ITPA." "Work on auditory association and grammatic closure." It is almost as mindless as teaching to materials. "What are you programming for Susie?" "I'm using DLM." "Yes, but what are you using them *for?*" "Oh."

A point to dwell upon. The end goal of an assessment should *never* be a score. Neither an IQ score, a mental age, nor a "psycholinguistic age" tells us anything particularly useful about a child, particularly a child who is developing atypically. A summary score — IQ, M.A., PLA, etc. — is the result of an amalgam; a combining of high and low scores obtained on samples of verbal, performance, motor, and graphomotor behavior. The end result is a summary score which frequently describes no child.

One needs to be clear about what the goals of an assessment are. For our purposes, assessments should be undertaken in order to sample enough behaviors, to elicit enough responses, to tap as many modalities as possible, in order to provide the most complete picture the state of the art permits. We need to know as much as possible about how and where the child functions and dysfunctions.

Some caveats: In the area of IQ testing, a frequent part of any complete evaluation, the Stanford-Binet is ubiquitous. Binet and his collaborators made a tremendous contribution to the field of individual differences,[7,38] and their work provided useful heuristic devices for some time after. Enough! It is time for retirement. The Stanford-Binet gives *only* summary scores. It is heavily loaded in language areas. When such a test is administered to a language-disordered child and is the sole criterion used, results are fairly predictible. The child will likely be seen as retarded or emotionally disturbed. No one test can or should be used in arriving at a diagnostic statement. We know that language-disordered children may have deficit areas other than language. We know that they have areas of intact function. We need to be able to separate these out as exquisitely as we can, not lose the discriminants by combining them.

How do we look at a variety of measures? How do we extract and present data so that they become useful information? In the absence of an appropriately standardized battery normed for a language disordered population, we'd best use what we have in the most judicious manner. The approach that we and our colleagues in Neuropsychology at North Shore University Hospital and at the Preschool Development Program have taken is based on several premises:

1. Behavior is a reflection of central nervous system activity. The nervous system functions systematically and dysfunctions systematically. It should therefore be possible to develop profiles, based on data, that reflect systematic patterns of function and dysfunction and will ultimately be related to brain function.

2. Selecting subtests, from standardized instruments wherever possible, will permit us to sample adequate subsets of behaviors. The more behaviors we sample, the better.

3. If a deficit is identified by one subtest, demonstrate it again with another. One swallow does not a summer make.

4. There are subsets of language disorders. Even at the current (low) level of knowledge in this area, it should be possible to discern systematic differences between children and among groups of children, using a profile analysis approach.

5. Children with a developmental delay in one area usually have more than one. Look beyond the "chief complaint."

At the Preschool Development Program, we have put together a first approximation to a battery composed of subtests taken from standardized instruments. These are listed in the Appendix, page 166. Our original selection was based on elusive "clinical judgement" and task analyses of subtest items. Essentially what we have done with the neuropsychologic test scores is to convert each into a z-score, then into a centile score. This was done so that all measures, regardless of the system of scoring on the individual test, can be compared to each other. The test data, based on forty, three- to five-year-old children were then subjected to factor and cluster analyses. Some of the results of this first round factor analysis, modified by clinical judgement, are presented in histogram form below.

This profile approach has proved to be useful to those working with children in terms of providing modality-specific information. It also serves as an excellent heuristic device in terms of generating hypotheses regarding brain-behavior relationships. We have applied the general approach to children of all ages and with a variety of disabilities and diagnoses. It seems a generally useful method which we plan to refine and expand as we increase our data bank.

We are also in the process of developing an assessment of linguistic competence, based on a good-sized normative population. The assessment, based on analyses of elicited and spontaneous language samples, will provide the information for making quantitative statements about the syntax, semantics and phonology of the preschool child. The model we are using is related to that elaborated by Doris Allen[1] and subsequently used in a study of seven- to twelve-year-old language-disordered children.[35] Our method for obtaining the spontaneous language sample was developed at the Preschool Development Program.[20] We have not as yet completed our analysis of the preschool language data. Some samples of the linguistic analyses completed on the school aged children are presented below. The paradigm is the same.

The factors represented in the neuropsychologic profiles represent our best judgement as to what subtests actually test. No subtest or group of subtests is really a pure measure of anything. We have grouped by what our clinical judgement and a first round factor analysis suggests. To review them briefly, *FM* is a fine motor factor, based on tasks such as bead stringing or peg placement. *GrM* taps graphomotor skills, based on the child's ability with paper and pencil tasks. It is noteworthy that every child we have screened for the preschool program over the past three years has shown deficits in fine or graphomotor function, typically in both. *AD* represents auditory discrimination, with relatively little cognitive content involved. *AM1* taps short-term auditory sequential memory, while *AM2* taps retrieval. *AC* represents tasks involving auditory input, requiring a verbal output with some cognitive content. *VD* represents rather straight-forward visual discrimination, match-to-sample ability. The *VSp* factor involves visual-spatial analysis and synthesis and appears to reflect aspects of constructional praxis. *VM1* represents visual short-term sequential memory, while *VM2* assesses visual memory for single stimuli. *VC* is analogous to the auditory conceptual tasks, except that here the input is visual. *A-V* represents the stimulus situation in which both auditory and visual channels are involved — the *multimodal* or *intersensory* input model.

There are many behaviors and constellations of behaviors not represented here and that await further analysis. What we have does give us a first approximation to functionally oriented test data analyses.

Figure 13–2 is a profile of a four-year-old boy, C.B., with a diagnosis of significant delay in language development. It is clear that other delays or disabilities are attendant, particularly in the

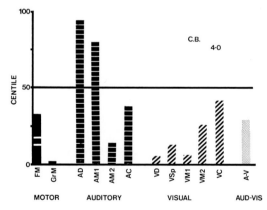

Figure 13-2. C.B. is the product of a thirty-six-week pregnancy. Birth-weight was 7 pounds. All milestones were slightly delayed. Neurological examination led to a diagnostic impression of maturational delay. EEG and audiological examinations were normal. C.B. appears to be an apraxic child with delayed motor, spatial planning, and sequencing skills. Auditory and visual receptive skills are relatively deficient.

visual areas. In this instance, relative strengths lie in the auditory area, apart from a problem in retrieval. Of a special interest is the lack of facilitation provided when both auditory and visual channels are simultaneously involved. Note, too, the deficits in the motor areas.

Figure 13–3, S.S., shows a rather different profile of a boy who is also considered language disordered. Here, the deficits clearly occur in the auditory area, directing one to a very different set of intervention strategies than those considered for C.B., above. Pairing the efficient visual channel with deficient auditory skills leads to a decrement in cognitive performance, indicated by comparing centiles obtained for the AC, VC, and AV factors.

One might characterize the sets of data presented in Figures 13–2 and 13–3 as representing left versus right hemisphere differences, suggesting that the nature of the observed behavioral deficits relate to relative efficiencies of right versus left brain. Although we are drawing on the adult model in terms of localization of specific functions, we have seen enough young children who

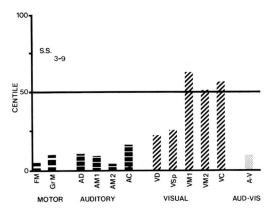

Figure 13-3. S.S. was born at six and one-half months with a birthweight of 3 pounds, 4 ounces. He was incubated and received oxygen. Motor milestones were age-appropriate. Single words were noted at eighteen months; phrases and sentences were delayed. Intelligibility is still poor. Neurological examination was essentially negative, except for oromotor findings (tongue thrust, drooling). EEG and audiological evaluations were negative. S.S. is seen as a child with a primary language disorder.

present with systematic patterns to warrant presentation of these data in support of a hypothesis arguing for more not less "hard wiring" early on, in language and in visual-perceptual domains. This position lends itself to programs of research concerned with the elucidation of developmental brain-behavior relationships in very young children.

Figure 13–4 presents the profile of a child who might easily be seen as retarded on the basis of a typical one session Stanford-Binet kind of evaluation. D.B. has significant oromotor deficits, including the presence of an oromotor apraxia, contributing to poor intelligibility. Motor skills are, in general, deficient. D.B.'s auditory skills are shown to be poor, with auditory cognitive function the highest of the group. Visual skills are poor as well, in terms of simple discrimination, visual-spatial function and memory, but he is able to solve problems on the basis of visual input and does so at an above average level. When the A-V tasks are presented, this child's circuits appear to "overload," and he seems unable to process and/or integrate incoming information.

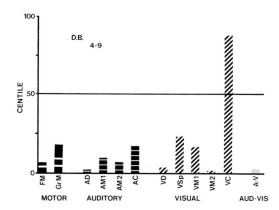

Figure 13-4. D.B. is the product of an uneventful pregnancy and delivery. All milestones were appropriately acquired. Audiological evaluations and EEG were reported to be normal. Neurological findings were essentially negative, except for the presence of oromotor deficits. Language has not been developed beyond the single-word or short-phrase level. Gesture language is excellent. D.B. is considered to have a primary language disorder.

In spite of his limited verbal skills, this little boy communicates extremely well via a sophisticated gesture language. We are planning to teach him manual communication, hypothesizing that this may serve as a facilitator in the acquisition of linguistic skills. Figures 13–5 and 13–6 present abbreviated neuropsychologic and linguistic profiles in two school-age children.[35] Because of the difference in ages, these neuropsychologic factors include different subtests than those used for the preschoolers. The subtests are listed in the Appendix, pages 167,168. The neuropsychologic factors are plotted on a 0 to 100 centile scale. It should be noted that the language analysis ranges from "deficit" to "average" (maximum on the graph), or from 0 to the 50th centile. In the absence of quantitative norms for most of the variables involved in the language analysis, one cannot determine how much "better" than average a given performance may be. The linguistic analysis, then, represents a combination of clinical judgement and data, translated into a set of scales which differentiate "normal" from "deficient" performance.

The semantic, syntactic, and phonologic factors are based on specific variables listed in the Appendix. The phonologic factor includes aspects of articulation, prosody, and voice. The data were also subjected to syntactic analysis, according to a tagmemic grammar called *sector analysis,* which allows for analyses of both syntactic function and syntactic form. It also allows for a determination of the range of semantic distinctions expressed by the child.[1]

Figure 13–5 indicates average IQs with the WISC performance scale and the Raven Coloured Progressive Matrices, a lower IQ on the Hiskey which, although also nonverbal, has language-loaded subtests. This eight-year-old, J.G., has visual functions which are reasonably good, except for nonlinguistic visual memory. Auditory skills, on the other hand, are practically nonexistent. The linguistic analysis indicates adequate phonologic skills and deficient syntax and semantics.

Figure 13–6 presents the profile of an extremely bright nine-year-old boy, J.D., whose visual cognitive skills are significantly above average. His auditory receptive skills are extremely de-

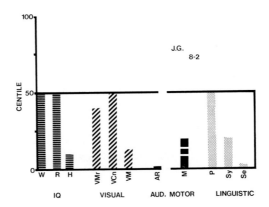

Figure 13-5. J.G. is the product of a normal pregnancy and delivery. All milestones were age-appropriate, except for language. Single words were not noted until eighteen months. Short sentences have only recently developed. Some echolalia is noted. EEG and audiological evaluations were negative. Results of the neurological examination indicated the presence of brain damage manifested by a mild left hemiparesis. Receptive deficits are present, but not as severe as the expressive deficits in this language-disordered child.

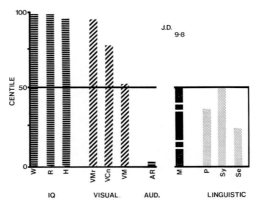

Figure 13-6. J.D. is the product of a normal pregnancy and delivery. Birth-weight was $9\frac{1}{2}$ pounds. Motor milestones were within normal limits. Language was significantly delayed; single words did not occur until two and one-half years. EEG, audiological, and neurological evaluations were essentially normal. This child is seen as having a primary language disorder.

ficient, as are his phonology and semantics. His verbal output, which is voluminous, is syntactically correct but conveys little meaning because of disordered semantic usage.

The figures have been presented in order to make several points: Patterns of function and dysfunction are typically systematic and can be conceptualized as reflecting differences in hemispheric efficiency; there are discernible differences among language disordered children on both neuropsychologic and linguistic measures. Subsets do, indeed, appear to exist and are important to identify. Intervention strategies must differ as the patterns of function and dysfunction differ among children, who represent subsets.

One area clearly in need of ongoing research is that concerned with continued delineation of systematic patterns and their relationship to the efficacy of alternate models of remediation. We are approaching the time when remedial or compensatory educational or rehabilitation methods should program "to the brain." This is being done to some extent, particularly in rehabilitation settings. It is our position that maximal gains can be affected in a nonrandom fashion only when knowledge of brain function and behavior, as acquired, is brought to bear on the development of remedial curricula, methods and materials, and intervention strategies at large.

APPENDIX

I. Tasks included in the factors. Preschool data.

A. *FM — Fine Motor*
Beads — H-N
Fine Motor I — LAP

B. *GrM — Graphomotor*
Draw-A-Design — McC
Geometric Design —
WPPSI
Fine Motor II — LAP

C. *AD — Auditory Discrimination*
Auditory Closure—ITPA
Auditory Memory —
ITPA
Sound Blending — ITPA

D. *AM1 — Auditory Memory 1 (sequential)*
Auditory Sequential
Memory — ITPA
Numerical Memory 1 —
McC
Verbal Memory — McC
Sentence Repetition —
WPPSI

E. *AM2 — Auditory Memory 2 (retrieval)*
Verbal Memory 2 — McC
Verbal Fluency — McC

F. *AC — Auditory-Cognitive*
Auditory Association —
ITPA
Auditory Reception —
ITPA
Opposite Analogies —
McC

G. *VD — Visual Discrimination*
Form Discrimination —
PTI
Picture Identification —
H-N

H. *VSp — Visual-Spatial*
Puzzle Solving — McC
Counting/Sorting—McC
Block Patterns — H-N
Block Designs — WPPSI

I. *VM1 — Visual Memory 1 (sequential)*
Tapping — McC
Visual Attention Span —
H-N
Memory for Color —
H-N
Visual Sequential Memory — ITPA

166

J. *VM2 — Visual Memory 2*
   (single item)
   Immediate Recall — PTI
K. *VC — Visual-Cognitive*
   Picture Association —
      H-N
   Visual Association —
      ITPA
   Visual Reception —
      ITPA

L. *A-V — Auditory-Visual*
   Cognitive
   Peabody Picture Vocabu-
      lary
   Information-Comprehen-
      sion — PTI
   Picture Vocabulary —
      PTI
   Grammatic Closure —
      ITPA

H-N = Hiskey-Nebraska Test of Learning Aptitude
LAP = Learning Accomplishment Profile
McC = McCarthy Scales of Children's Abilities
WPPSI = Wechsler Preschool and Primary Scale of Intelligence
ITPA = Illinois Test of Psycholinguistic Abilities
PTI = Pictorial Test of Intelligence

II. Tasks included in the Rapin et al.[35] factors.

   A. *IQ*
      W = Wechsler Intelligence Scale for Children (Perform-
         ance Scales)
      R = Raven Coloured Progressive Matrices
      H-N = Hiskey-Nebraska Test of Learning Aptitude

   B. *VMr — Visual-Motor*
      Visual Closure — ITPA
      Embedded Figures — Spreen-Benton
      Mazes — WISC
      Coding — WISC
      Drawing Completion — H-N
      Benton C — Benton Visual Retention Test

   C. *VCn — Visual Constructional*
      Picture Arrangement — WISC
      Object Assembly — WISC
      Block Design — WISC
      Coding — WISC
      Block Patterns — H-N
      Paper Folding — H-N

D. *VM — Visual Memory (nonlinguistic)*
 Memory for Color — H-N
 Bead Patterns — H-N
 Paper Folding — H-N
 Visual Sequential Memory — ITPA
 Coding — WISC
 Benton A — Benton Visual Retention Test

E. *AR — Auditory Reception*
 Auditory Reception — ITPA
 Auditory Association — ITPA
 Grammatic Closure — ITPA
 Auditory Closure — ITPA

F. *M — Motor*
 Motor Findings — neurologic examination
 Oromotor Function — oromotor examination
 Verbal Diadochokinesis — oromotor examination
 Peg Placement — Purdue Pegboard

G. *P — Phonology*
 Sound Blending — ITPA
 Substitutions
 Omissions
 Distortions   } Analysis of taped language sample
 Nasality

H. *Sy — Syntax*
 Prepositions
 General syntax
 Mean Length of Utterance
 Tense
 - - - - - - ing   } Analysis of taped language sample
 Determinants
 Syntax
 Possessive

I. *Se — Semantics*
 Semantic integration   } Analysis of taped language sample
 Focus

REFERENCES

1. Allen, D.: *The Development of Predication in Child Language.* Unpublished dissertation. Teacher's College, Columbia University, 1973.
2. Bartak, L., Rutter, M., and Cox, A.: A comparative study of infantile autism and specific developmental receptive language disorder. I. The children. *Br J Psychiatry, 126:*230-237, 1975.
3. Bender, L.: A longitudinal study of schizophrenic children with autism. *Hosp Community Psychiatry, 20:*230-237, 1969.
4. Bergman, P. and Escalona, S.K.: Unusual sensitivities in very young children. *Psychoanal Study Child, 3,4:*333-353, 1949.
5. Berry, M.F.: *Language Disorders of Children.* New York, Appleton, 1969, p. 6.
6. Berry, P.: *Language and Communication in the Mentally Handicapped.* Baltimore, Univ Park, 1976.
7. Binet, A. and Simon, T.: Méthodes nouvelles pour le diagnostic du niveau intellectuel des anormaux. *Annee Psychol, 11:*191-244, 1905.
8. Brown, R.: *A First Language.* Cambridge, Harvard U Pr, 1973.
9. Churchill, D.W.: The relation of infantile autism and early childhood schizophrenia to developmental language disorders of childhood. *J Autism Child Schizo, 2:*182-197, 1972.
10. Clancy, H. and Rendle-Short, J.: Infantile autism—A problem of communication. *Aust J Occup Ther, 15:3,* 1968.
11. Clancy, H., Dugdale, A., and Rendle-Short, J.: The diagnosis of infantile autism. *Dev Med Child Neurol, 11:*432-442, 1969.
12. Condon, W.S.: Multiple response to sound in dysfunctional children. *J Autism Child Schizo, 5:*37-56, 1975.
13. Creak, M.: Schizophrenic syndrome in childhood. Progress report of a working party. *Br Med J, 2:*890, 1961.
14. Creak, M.: Schizophrenic syndrome in childhood. Further progress report of a working party. *Dev Med Child Neurol, 4:*530, 1964.
15. Critchley, M.: *Developmental Dyslexia.* Springfield, Thomas, 1964.
16. Dalby, M.A.: *Air Studies in Language-Retarded Children. Evidence of Early Lateralization of Language Function.* Presented at The First International Congress of Child Neurology, Toronto, October, 1975.
17. De Myer, M.K. et al.: Prognosis in autism: A follow-up study. *J Autism Child Schizo, 3:*199-246, 1973.
18. Fish, B.: Longitudinal observation of biological deviations in a schizophrenic infant. *Am J Psychiatry, 116:*25-31, 1959.
19. Fish, B.: Involvement of the central nervous system in infants with schizophrenia. *Arch Neurol, 2:*115-121, 1960.
20. Goore, D., Allen, D., and Wilson, B.C.: *The Use of the Film Loop in Eliciting Spontaneous Speech.* Unpublished manuscript.
21. Griffith, R.J. and Ritvo, E.R.: Echolalia: Concerning the dynamics of

the syndrome. *J Am Acad Child Psychiatry, 6:*184-193, 1967.

22. Hauser, S.L., DeLong, R., and Rosman, N.P.: Pneumographic findings in the infantile autism syndrome: A correlation with temporal lobe disease. *Brain, 98:*667-688, 1975.

23. Holt, K. (Ed.): *Movement and Child Development.* Clinics in Developmental Medicine No. 55. Spastics International Medical Publications. London, William Heinemann Medical Books Ltd.; Philadelphia, Lippincott, 1975.

24. Kalverboer, A.F.: *A Neurobehavioral Study in Pre-School Children.* Clinics in Developmental Medicine No. 54. Spastics International Publications. London, William Heinemann Medical Books Ltd.; Philadelphia, Lippincott, 1975.

25. Kanner, L.: Early infantile autism. *J Pediatr, 25:*211-217, 1944.

26. Lackner, J.R.: A developmental study of language behavior in retarded children. *Neuropsychologia, 6:*301-320, 1968.

27. Lenneberg, E.: *Biological Foundations of Language.* New York, Wiley, 1967.

28. Mahler, M.S.: On early infantile psychosis. The symbiotic and autistic syndrome. *J Am Acad Child Psychiatry, 4:*554-568, 1965.

29. McNeill, D.: *The Acquisition of Language: The Study of Developmental Psycholinguistics.* New York, Harper & Row, 1970.

30. Morehead, D.M. and Morehead, A.: From signal to sign: A Piagetian view of thought and language during the first two years. In Schieffelbusch, R.L. and Lloyd, L.L. (Eds.): *Language Perspectives—Acquisition, Retardation and Intervention.* Baltimore, Univ Park, 1974, pp. 153-190.

31. Ornitz, E.M.: Childhood autism—A disorder of sensorimotor integration. In Rutter, M. (Ed.): *Infantile autism: Concepts, Characteristics and Treatment.* London, Churchill, 1971.

32. Ornitz, E.M. and Ritvo, E.R.: Perceptual inconstancy in early infantile autism. *Arch Gen Psychiatry, 18:*76-98, 1960.

33. Piaget, J.: Le language et les opérations intellectuelles. In *Problèmes de Psycholinguistiques.* Symposium de L'association de Psychologie Scientifique de Langue Française. Paris, Presses Universitaires de France, 1963.

34. Rapin, I. and Wilson, B.C.: *Children with Developmental Language Disability: Neurologic Aspects and Assessment.* Acad Pr, in press.

35. Rapin, I., Wilson, B.C., Wilson, J.J., Allen, D., and Miller, B.: *Developmental Language Disabilities: A Multi-Disciplinary View.* In preparation.

36. Ritvo, E.R. (Ed.): *Autism, Diagnoses, Current Research and Management.* New York, Spectrum, Prentice-Hall, 1976.

37. Rutter, M., Bartak, L., and Newman, S.: Autism—A central disorder of cognition and language? In Rutter, M. (Ed.): *Infantile Autism: Con-*

cepts, Characteristics and Treatment. London, Churchill, 1970.

38. Terman, L.M.: *The Measurement of Intelligence.* Boston, Houghton-Mifflin, 1916.

39. Towen, C.L. and Prechtl, H.F.R.: *The Neurological Examination of the Child with Minor Nervous Dysfunction.* Clinics in Developmental Medicine No. 38. Spastics International Medical Publications. London, William Heinemann Medical Books, Ltd.; Philadelphia, Lippincott, 1970.

40. Wilson, J.J., Rapin, I., Wilson, B.C., and VanDenburg, F.V.: Neuropsychologic function of children with severe hearing impairment. *J Speech Hear Res, 18:*634-652, 1975.

CHAPTER 14.

A COMMUNITY PSYCHOLOGY APPROACH TO DEVELOPMENTAL DISABILITIES

RICHARD M. COHEN, Ph.D.

WHILE developmental disabilities would appear to be relatively untouched by the community psychology/community mental health approach, conceptualizations[3,4,6] of conditions such as autism and mental retardation within a developmental, rather than a medical/disease model, are in keeping with the philosophical and theoretical thrust of the "community" movement. The *community* approach emphasizes conceptualizations, stressing avoidance of isolation of individuals through labeling, equal importance (if not greater) of environmental factors with intrapsychic and internal determinants (influences) of disability, and some treatment variant based on the principles of normalization, e.g. mainstreaming, community-based residences. These community approaches thus would agree with a view that developmental differences reflect differences in rate and limits rather than specific etiological (physiological, psychological, or cognitive) defect that is of greater importance than the rate differences.

Central to a community psychology approach to the developmentally disabled would be efforts to maintain such an individual in a social system as close to the "norm" as possible or to intervene with the existing systems in ways that permit greater inclusion in the mainstream of the developmentally disabled individual.

Flowing from this approach, program emphases, as suggested by Menolascino,[3,4] for the developmentally disabled might (1) allow the individual to increasingly develop control over his/her environment, (2) increase the complexity of his/her behavior, (3) extend his/her repertoire of interpersonal skills, and (4) maximize his/her humanization. The kinds of systems interven-

172

tion indicated to achieve these aims are the focus of this paper and will be considered shortly.

The priorities of The Joint Commission on Mental Health of Children also reflect a community model. The recommendations of the commission reflect the following community psychology emphases:

Prevention

1. The need for preventative services
2. Emphasis on the period from conception to age three
3. The developmental approach

Social Environmental Factors

1. Primacy of the family
2. Deviance occurs within a social context
3. Priorities for, but not segregation of, the poor

Systems Emphasis

1. The need for comprehensive services
2. Integration of mental health and mental retardation programs
3. A need for research and demonstration programs

For an elaboration of, and specific recommendations relevant to the priorities, the reader is referred to the full report.[2] For purposes here, I will focus on the issue of the system emphasis as indicated above and the levels of intervention to be achieved within the varying systems suggested by the community psychology model.

Briefly, the systems approach may be an analysis of a system as circumscribed as a marital or family unit to the system of an entire population. A system may also refer to the interaction between an individual and a community institution. According to Murrell,[3] the important concepts are —

1. THE COMPLEX PERSON* ASSUMPTION: "People are motivated according to their specific individual experiences, expectancies and values which are developed over a lifetime of en-

*Complex-man in Murrell.

countering and attempting to master problems." This would apply to the developmentally disabled. Often this assumption is omitted, and the developmentally disabled are seen as without expectations, values, needs, etc.

2. THE PROBLEM AREA CONCEPT: For each individual, "there are a number of areas of particular psychosocial concern for him in which he is trying to accomplish some end. In order to obtain this end the individual must engage his environment." This seems to be the *sine qua non* for the developmentally disabled. However, rather than the positive growth sense indicated here, the problem area is too frequently interpreted in the perjorative, defect sense.

3. THE CONCEPT OF SYSTEM ASSIGNMENT: "The specific individual in a particular social system has a tailored social niche constructed from the social system, that is, expectations and tasks." The "goodness of fit" between individuals and system assignment reflects success of the social system in providing opportunity for individual problem management. This would apply to the limited assignments available to the developmentally disabled and the need to broaden these. A further issue relevant to this point would be the continual utilization of stereotypic categorizations and positions within the system for the developmentally disabled rather than attempting to achieve a "goodness of fit" between the particular individual and the possibilities within the systems.

4. THE CONCEPT OF INTERSYSTEM ACCOMMODATION: This refers to the compatability among the different social systems in their system assignments for the same individual. Thus, for the developmentally disabled individual, this would refer to the demands of the systems, such as the family, the responsible agency, and the school. Are the demands consistent or conflictual? What effect does this have upon the developmentally disabled person?

As caregivers, we are all involved in intervention to introduce change. Noting, but eschewing for our purposes here, the issue of the value judgments involved in determining what individual and system intervention one decides to attempt to accomplish, I will review the six levels of interventions (suggested by Murrell) and see how this might apply to the developmentally disabled.

Level 1: Individual Relocation

The basis for this intervention is a lack of "goodness of fit" between the individual and the place within the social system. In the traditional utilization of this level of intervention, placement in institutions has been the primary modality. In the community psychological approach, movement, not to institutions, but to smaller residences, foster homes, and respite care would reflect this intervention.

Level 2: Individual Intervention

The goal of this level of intervention is to change or add to the individual's native resources. Many of the traditional approaches to the developmentally disabled are included in this level of intervention: special education, supportive psychotherapy, visual-motor stimulation, chemotherapy. More recent individual interventions would include behavior modification techniques, biofeedback, and sex therapy, etc.

Level 3: Population Interventions

This intervention aims at preventative interventions. The eventual goal of this level of intervention is to modify the environment. Thus, public dissemination of information on such topics as nutrition, genetic counseling, and parent education are examples of this level of intervention. Direct workshops with parents to deal with potential crisis areas with the developmentally disabled such as death or sexual needs are further examples.

Level 4: Social System Intervention

There are several foci of this intervention. In one, the aim is to make changes in the caretaker's skills and attitudes in the particular system that one is addressing. A second goal is to increase the "assignment latitude" and/or variety available to the developmentally disabled within the system. Examples of the former are educating personnel in a state training school in behavior modification techniques or humanistic education techniques, etc., with the goal of impacting upon the entire system. An example of increasing the assignment latitude working within the educational system to provide increased options for the developmentally disabled youngster, rather than having them stereotypically placed.

A final kind of a system intervention is the design of an entirely new system to handle the problem of developmental disabilities, rather than utilizing the current system and making changes. This latter intervention is clearly the most difficult to achieve, because of the inherent resistance to system change from existing systems.

Level 5: Intersystem Intervention

There are several levels at which an intersystem intervention may be made. At the level of intersystem coordination, one thinks of liaison workers; when youngsters are discharged from an institution, there is an advocate from the institution who helps the parents and developmentally disabled child negotiate, return to the community, placement within the educational system, contact with appropriate community agencies, etc.

At another level, intersystem coordination programs are reflected in local, county, or statewide organizations in which the goal is facilitation of coordination between the various parts of the system. Thus for example, in New York City, The Federation of Mental Health, Mental Retardation, and Alcoholism Services provides, on the borough and citywide level, an arena for discussion of relevant issues and clarification of coordinating functions. Placement for the "hard-to-place youngster" is found through committees focused upon Mental Retardation and Child Mental Health, and subcommittees dealing with issues of implementation. Through committees about residences and school/ agency coordination among other committees, the goal is to enable various components of the system to work in a cooperative fashion.

A final method of intersystem intervention is that of community action, in which one attempts to involve members of the community, e.g. an advisory board, for an interchange between community and professionals relevant to the problems of developmental disability.

Level 6: Network Intervention

While network interventions are rare, they refer to community-wide efforts to improve environments, such as participation in urban and regional planning committees to make the planner aware of the special needs of developmentally disabled youngsters, whether this is the need for ramps in buildings, elevator facilities, electric-eye opening doors, etc. This level would involve the spectrum of institutions and community resources and education programs as part of all planning that is attempted. An example, again from New York, is the Metropolitan Placement Unit of the State of New York. The mandate of this unit is community placement of children to be deinstitutionalized as part of the Willowbrook consent decree. Because of community resistance network intervention is necessary at the comprehensive health planning level, the civic association level, the political (borough president, city councilman) level. Clearly the complexity of these issues makes this a very difficult and time-consuming kind of intervention.

Utilizing the community psychology and systems approach, several aspects of work with the developmentally disabled are placed in perspective:

1. One must approach the developmentally disabled from multilevels — an individual approach is no longer sufficient.

2. Much must still be done to intervene with the general stereotypes of the developmentally disabled. The fears and anxieties must be met with controlled contact, media presentations and early education.

3. The system (s) that deal (s) with the developmentally disabled must cease isolation from other systems and work through mutual cooperation.

4. Continued input on the network and intersystem levels must be pursued as these continue to be the source of funding and political support.

REFERENCES

1. Gruen, G. and Zigler, E.: Expectancy of success and the probability learning of middle-class, lower-class and retarded children. In Chess, S. and

Thomas, A. (Eds.): *Annual Progress in Child Psychiatry and Child Development 1969*. New York, Brunner-Mazel, 1969, pp. 352-368.

2. Joint Commission on Mental Health of Children: *Mental Health: From Infancy Through Adolescence*. New York, Harper & Row, 1973.

3. Menolascino, F.J.: Community psychiatry and mental retardation. In Bellak, L. and Barten, H.H. (Eds.): *Progress in Community Mental Health*. New York, Brunner-Mazel, 1975, vol. III, pp. 140-178.

4. Menolascino, F.J.: Emotional disturbances in mentally retarded children. In Chess, S. and Thomas, A. (Eds.): *Annual Progress in Child Psychiatry and Child Development, 1970*. New York, Brunner-Mazel, 1970, pp. 376-389.

5. Murrell, S.A.: *Community Psychology and Social Systems*. New York, Behavioral Pub, 1973, chapter 6.

6. Rutter, M.: Concepts of autism: A review of research. In Chess, S. and Thomas, A. (Eds.): *Annual Progress in Child Psychiatry and Child Development, 1969*. New York, Brunner-Mazel, 1969, pp. 379-410.

The interested reader is also referred both to *Children Today,* a publication of the U.S. Department of Health, Education and Welfare/OHD/OCD and the Children's Bureau and to the volumes of the Joint Commission on Mental Health of Children: *Crisis in Child Mental Health; The Mental Health of Children: Services, Research and Manpower;* and *Social Change and the Mental Health of Children.*

AUTHOR INDEX

SUBJECT INDEX